Charlou's
FIVE-FINGER
PUPPETS
AND STUFFED TOYS

Charlou's FIVE-FINGER PUPPETS AND STUFFED TOYS

Charlou Baker Dolan

Sedgewood® Press
New York, N.Y.

This book is dedicated to my father
WELDON NICHOLAS BAKER
who always thought I could do
anything I set out to do.

Very special thanks to the children and adults who helped show off the puppets:

Charlotte Baker
Charlou Dolan
Dan Dolan
Meg Dolan
Tom Dolan
Zak Dolan
Spencer Galsworth
Jeffrey Guiliano
Hidde Heydendael
Cheryl Keller
Nadine Milligan

Nicholas Rice
Lauren Beth Schachter
David Stickley
Jan Straka
Michael Sue Low Chee
Nicole Sue Low Chee
Kerry Travis
Molly Van Note
Christy Volosin
John Volosin Jr.
Jenny Warren

For Sedgewood® Press:
Director: Elizabeth P. Rice
Associate Editor: Leslie Gilbert
Project Editor: Ciba Vaughan
Production Manager: Bill Rose
Book Design: Remo Cosentino
Photography: Thomas Famighetti
Black and White Photography: Suzi Alexander

Distributed by Macmillan Publishing Company, a division of Macmillan, Inc.

ISBN: 0-02-496820-X
Library of Congress Catalog Card Number: 86-61600

Printed in the United States of America

10 9 8 7 6 5 4 3 2 1

Contents

Introduction

I grew up with homemade stuffed animals, most of which were hand-me-downs, and many of which I, in turn, handed down to my younger brother and sister. When my first son was born, he had a teddy bear waiting for him when he came home from the hospital, and I assumed that he would play with it for many happy years to come. Unfortunately, the bear lost its leg very quickly. I figured I could make sturdier stuffed toys for my son myself.

Before long, people were not only admiring the animals I made for my sons (by this time there were two), but they were also asking me to make some for their children. That, basically, is how I got started in the stuffed toy business.

My main problem was finding good patterns. Too many patterns didn't fit together well, or required horrendous amounts of hand-sewing. Other patterns went together all right, but turned out to be sort of ho-hum animals. After five years of making stuffed animals and puppets (about 3,000 of them), I had learned a lot. I decided to start designing my own patterns.

I also started teaching other people to make stuffed toys. In the process, I realized how many things I could teach them that I had learned the hard way—some things I had discovered by accident, some through research, some through tips from friends, and some through sheer brilliant reasoning! I passed these little tricks on to my classes and my students became very good toymakers, too.

My classes also taught me some things. I learned that if you give someone pages and pages of instructions before she starts working on a project, either she won't bother to read the instructions, or she will read and promptly forget them. The best way to teach someone to make a stuffed toy is to let her make a stuffed toy, and give instructions each step of the way.

That's the rationale behind this book. You will learn techniques by making a simple Prairie Dog five-finger puppet. At each step I will tell you everything you need to know to do that particular step. If you work through every step of the Prairie Dog—reading each step all the way through before you do it—you should then be able to make any project in this book.

The book is divided into seven sections. In general, the puppets become more difficult to make as you progress through the book. Section I includes detailed instructions for the Prairie Dog. Please make at least one Prairie Dog before you try any of the others! The Prairie Dog will teach you all the basics.

Section II contains other simple puppets—such as the Squirrel, Bear, Lion and Rabbit—made like the Prairie Dog but with slight variations. I recommend making two or three puppets from this section before you go on to other sections, to reinforce what you learned when making the Prairie Dog.

Section III features puppets—like the Koala, Monkey, and Raccoon—which have changes in the method of head construction, and are a bit more complicated. In Section IV, the puppets have changes in the body construction and are even more complex. This is especially true for the Skunk—save this one for the day when you're feeling particularly competent, determined, and ambitious.

Section V has my two favorite puppets. They are paired together at the end because they both have flat feet (instead of rounded ones), and because I think they are the best puppets in the book—and one should always save the best for last.

Section VI contains one general, all-purpose stuffed animal body. One body and a few variations is all you get; but that's all you need to turn any of the five-finger puppets into stuffed animals.

Finally, Section VII contains full-size patterns for all the puppets. Many of the basic pattern pieces are used for more than one puppet, so the pieces are numbered for easy reference.

These puppets and stuffed animals have been an overwhelming success wherever I've taken them—from the Ozarks Farmers Market to Taiwan. After you make your first one, I'm sure you'll be hooked on them too.

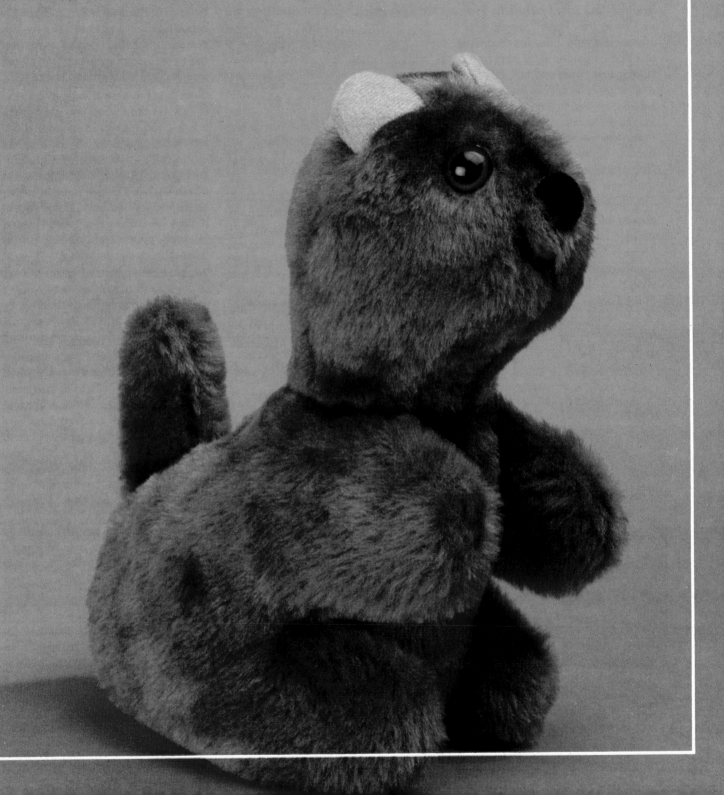

Since it is easier to sew the curve correctly when you are starting a seam than it is when you are ending a seam, have the neck to your right when you pin, and then you will start sewing at the neck. (This works whether you are right-handed or left-handed.) If you hold the pieces the same way each time you pin them, your hands will develop a certain dexterity that allows you to pin quickly and accurately.

16. Trim the seam allowance at J and K, as indicated by the dotted lines on the pattern.

Trimming the seam allowance to $\frac{1}{8}''$ gives the curve flexibility without weakening the seam as clipping the curves would do. If you accidentally trim away too much of the seam allowance, re-stitch the area that is too narrow—but just to $\frac{1}{8}''$ from the new edge.

17. Pin and sew the head to the body from M to C to M.

The head should still be right side out and the body wrong side out. Tuck the head down inside the body and hold the body towards you as you pin. You will be sewing inside the neck (see Figure 15). Match up the center front seam with notch C, and pin. Match the corners at M, and pin them. Note that J and H *do not* match.

Ease the material in between to fit, and pin it. The bottom edge of the head and the neck edge of the body are actually the same length (if you stitched your seam allowances carefully), but there will seem to be too much material on the inside and not enough on the outside. This is because the bulk of the fur makes the inside curve much smaller than the outside curve. Once you pin the edges evenly, the presser foot will mash things down quite nicely. Now, aren't you glad you left the head back seam partly open?!

18. Turn the head wrong side out again.

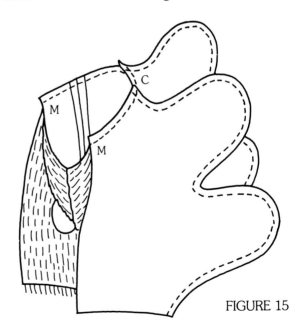

FIGURE 15

The whole puppet is now wrong side out.

19. Pin and sew the tail.

Pin and stitch the tail, leaving the straight edge open. After sewing, trim away half the seam allowance, leaving ⅛″.

Turn the tail right side out and stuff it very lightly with polyester stuffing. Use very small pieces of stuffing and push each one all the way to the end. When you think it is stuffed enough (it doesn't take much—the tail should be soft), place a pin parallel to the opening, and about ⅝″ from the raw edges. This pin holds the stuffing out of the way while you sew the tail in the seam. Now sew across the opening, about ⅛″ from the edge.

Note: If you take more than a ¼″ seam allowance when you sew the tail, you will find it very hard to turn the tail right side out.

20. Pin and sew the tail to one body back at N.

Match the lower edge of the tail (N) to notch N on one side of the body back. Pin and sew the tail about ⅛″ from the edge. It is easier to have the tail towards you when you pin and the body back facing up when you sew. I always pin it with the opening to the right (see Figure 16). Using this method, when I sew I am starting at the opening and sewing towards the head.

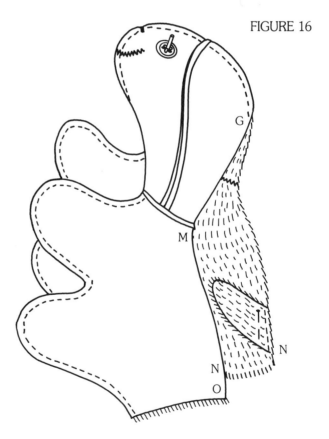

FIGURE 16

21. Pin and sew the back seam from G to M to O.

You need to have the side without the tail towards you when you pin, and face down when you sew. That way you can prevent any fabric from folding over and getting caught in the seam. After sewing the back seam, remove the pin from the tail.

22. Turn the puppet right side out.

Push the head down into the body by pushing the top of the head down through the neck opening. Then poke the legs into the body. Then push the head the rest of the way out of the body.

If this is hard on your fingers, make or buy a stuffing stick (useful later for making stuffed animals). A stuffing stick is a dowel about ⅝" in diameter and about 1' long. The handle of a wooden spoon also makes a good stuffing stick.

23. Stuff the head.

If you fill a balloon with air, the air pushes out equally in all directions. Unfortunately, stuffing doesn't work that way. If you push stuffing through the neck opening into the head, it will not spread out equally in all directions. Therefore, if you want stuffing in the nose you have to *push* it into the nose. If you want stuffing in the cheeks you have to *push* it into the cheeks.

Use small amounts of stuffing (How small is small? If you squeeze a "small amount" together as much as you can, it will be about the size of a large marble). Polyester stuffing is best—it is lighter than cotton batting or shredded fabric. Try to shape the head as you go, pushing stuffing out into the cheeks, the back of the head, the nose, etc.

Make sure that the stuffing doesn't push the eye pegs over sideways (this will make the eyes look weird). Work the stuffing in around the eyes.

Stuff the head firmly but not hard, so that it has a nice shape. Leave room in the chin, right along the seam, for your middle finger. Try the puppet on and make sure your finger is comfortable. If it's a tight squeeze, pull out a little stuffing until the fit is right.

It should take about ¾ oz. of stuffing for each puppet. I stuffed one of each of the 21 puppets and used almost exactly 16 oz. (one pound). If you stuff the simple puppets with smallish tails, you will be able to stuff more than 21 puppets with each pound of stuffing. If you stuff puppets that require more than average amounts of stuffing, such as the turtle (and its shell), the ram (and its horns), or the skunk (and its tail), you will stuff fewer than 21 puppets with each pound of stuffing.

24. Play with the puppet.

To put the puppet on, put your middle finger in the chin and your other fingers in the four legs. Your thumb and little finger will be in the hind legs.

Practice making the Prairie Dog scratch his head, hide his head in his paws, wave at you, crawl up your arm, grab your finger, nuzzle your neck, wrestle with another puppet, etc.

Helpful Hint: Fur is quite bulky to store. Egg crate boxes (available at grocery stores) are a convenient size for fur, and have hand holes at the ends which make them easy to carry. You can also stack them up, and they take up little room that way. Of course, the fur you want is always in the bottom box!

II. OTHER SIMPLE PUPPETS

Squirrel

I raised a baby squirrel once. They make marvelous pets. They're affectionate and lots of fun to play with when they are little.

I learned why squirrels can climb down trees easily. A squirrel has four little hands, with separate fingers, so he can grab onto telephone wires when he runs across them. But the real trick is that a squirrel can rotate his ankles and turn his feet completely around so that his claws dig into the tree trunk just as well when he is coming down as when he is going up!

Materials

BODY: Short pile ($3/16''$–$1/4''$) to medium pile ($5/16''$–$1/2''$) fur in any squirrel color, such as beige, brown, rust, or gray. The squirrel looks best in $1/4''$ fur.

EARS: Velour that coordinates well with the color of the fur.

TAIL: Shaggy fur to coordinate with the body fur. (If the shag is too thick—not too long, that doesn't matter—you will have a real struggle turning the tail right side out.)

NOSE: Small black ball fringe ($1/2''$).

EYES: 15 mm crystal eyes (brown for beige, brown, and rust squirrels, blue or brown for gray squirrels).

STUFFING: About $3/4$ oz. of polyester stuffing.

Because the shag furs are much harder to find than the shorter furs, it is best to find the shag fur first and then get short fur to coordinate with it. If you can't find any suitable shag, you can use fantasy fur (also called craft fur), which is sold at a lot of discount stores and craft supply shops. I don't like to use it if I can help it, because it doesn't wear as well as the other shags, and gets tired-looking sooner.

1. Trace and cut out the necessary pattern pieces.

For the squirrel you will need to trace pattern pieces 1, 2, 3, 4, 6, and 7 from Section VII. Cut patterns from sturdy paper or cardboard. Transfer all markings.

2. Trace around the patterns on the back of the fur.

For the Squirrel you will need to draw:

On the short fur:

Piece 1 (Body Back)—one right and one left

Piece 2 (Body Front)—one

Piece 3 (Head Front)—one right and one left

Piece 4 (Head Back)—one right and one left

On the shag fur:

Piece 7 (Tail)—one right and one left

3. Cut out the fur pieces.

Remember: Do not cut out the notches or the mouth lines.

4. Cut out the velour pieces.

You will need to pin and cut out:

Piece 6 (Ear)—four (two pairs)

Remember: Velour has a nap, so make sure you have the nap running in the same direction on both pairs of ears.

5. Zig-zag stitch the mouth lines on the head fronts, starting at A.

6. Pin and sew the head fronts together from B to C.

Remember: Be very careful to line up the mouths so that they come together in *exactly* the same place. Check the seam after you sew it, to make sure the mouth is right.

7. Sew on a ball-fringe nose at D.

8. Pin and sew the ears.

Trim seams and turn ears right side out. Stay-stitch across the bottom of each ear.

9. Sew the ears to each side of the

head front between notches E and F.

10. Insert the eyes.

11. Pin and sew the head backs together from B to G.

12. Pin and sew the head front to the head back from H to B to H. Turn head right side out and set aside.

13. Pin and sew the body backs to the body front from J to K to L.

14. Trim the seam allowance at J and K, as indicated by the dotted lines on the pattern.

15. Pin and sew the head to the body from M to C to M.

Remember: For this step, the head should be right side out and tucked down inside the body (which is wrong side out), so that the pile sides of the fur are together.

16. Turn the head wrong side out again.

17. Pin and sew the tail.

Pin and sew the tails together from P to Q and from N to Q (see Figure 1). Then with the top of the tail facing towards you, bring the Q's together and pin from R to Q to R (see Figure 2). Remember to tuck fur into the seam as you pin.

With the top of the tail face down on the machine, sew across the end of the tail from R to Q to R. Now, turn the tail right side out—this sounds easy, but it isn't. Start at the closed end of the tail and push it through the open end. Don't try to fold the open end back over the rest of the tail. Stuff the tail lightly. Use a pin parallel to the open end to hold the stuffing out of the way of the seam.

18. Pin and sew the tail to one body back, matching N's.

19. Pin and sew the back seam from G to M to O.

20. Turn the puppet right side out.

21. Stuff the head.

22. Play with the puppet.

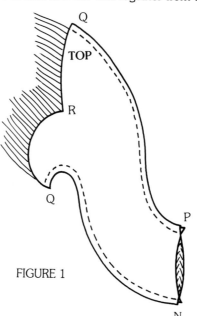

FIGURE 1

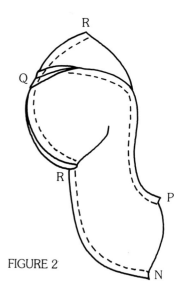

FIGURE 2

Bear

I usually make bears from ³⁄₈" or ¹⁄₂" plush fur. Sometimes though, I use a ⁷⁄₈" pile for an extra-fluffy bear. If you decide to use a longer pile fur, make sure it is soft and silky or it won't work.

Materials

BODY: Short pile (³⁄₁₆"–¹⁄₄") to medium pile (⁵⁄₁₆"–¹⁄₂") fur in any bear color (brown, black—or white if you want to make a Polar Bear). The Bears are most appealing when they are made out of plush fur. Plush fur has two characteristics that distinguish it from regular fake furs. First, it is quite dense, so the fibers stick up from the fabric, rather than lying flat. Second, the fibers are shiny and soft. Velvet is an example of a plush fabric, but plush furs are much denser than velvets. (Because of the density, plushes longer than ¹⁄₂" become impossible to sew, and are used mostly for rugs and bedspreads.)

NOSE: Small black ball fringe (¹⁄₂").

EYES: 15 mm crystal eyes, brown for black or brown bears, and blue for polar bears.

STUFFING: About ³⁄₄ oz. of polyester stuffing.

1. Trace and cut out the necessary pattern pieces.

For the Bear you will need pattern pieces 1, 2, 8, 9, and 10 from Section VII. Cut patterns from sturdy paper or cardboard. Transfer all markings.

2. Trace around the patterns on the back of the fur.

For the Bear you will need to draw:

Piece 1 (Body Back)—one right and one left

Piece 2 (Body Front)—one

Piece 8 (Head Front)—one right and one left

Piece 9 (Head Back)—one right and one left

Piece 10 (Ear)—four (two pairs)

For black or brown fur you will need to use the white ball-point fabric paint.

3. Cut out the fur pieces.

Remember: Do not cut out the notches or the mouth lines.

4. Zig-zag stitch the mouth lines on the head fronts, starting at A.

5. Pin and sew the head fronts together from B to C.

Remember: Be very careful to line up the mouths so that they come together exactly. Check the seam after you sew it, to make sure that the mouth is all right.

6. Sew on a ball-fringe nose at D.

7. Pin and sew the ears.

8. Sew the ears to the head front between notches E and F.

I have to admit that with the heavier plushes, this step and Step 11 tend to be real needle-breakers. But if you can get past these steps, you are home free for the Bear puppets!

9. Insert the eyes.

10. Pin and sew the head backs together from B to G.

11. Pin and sew the head front to the head back from H to B to H. Turn head right side out and set aside.

12. Pin and sew the body backs to the body front from J to K to L.

13. Trim the seam allowance at J and K, as indicated by the dotted lines on the pattern.

14. Pin and sew the head to the body from M to C to M.

Remember: The head should be right side out and tucked down inside the body (which is wrong side out), so that the pile sides of the fur are facing.

15. Turn the head wrong side out again.

16. Pin and sew the back seam from G to M to O.

17. Turn the puppet right side out.

18. Stuff the head.

19. Play with the puppet.

Rabbit

You don't have to wait for Easter to make rabbit puppets. The best thing about rabbits is that they come in so many different colors. I've made them in brown, gray, black, and the perennial favorite: white with a pink pompon tail.

Materials

BODY: Short pile ($\frac{3}{16}''$–$\frac{1}{4}''$) to medium pile ($\frac{5}{16}''$–$\frac{1}{2}''$) fur in any rabbit color (white, beige, brown, gray, spotted).

EAR LININGS: Velour that coordinates with the fur. For white Rabbits use pink.

NOSE: Small black ball fringe ($\frac{1}{2}''$). For white Rabbits use pink.

EYES: 15 mm crystal eyes in a color that looks good with the fur. For white Rabbits use pink.

TAIL: $3''$ pompon. Use pink for white Rabbits, white for all other color Rabbits. (For the pompon tails I use the pompons sold in card shops that go with yarn gift ties. You can make your own, but the ones in the stores are made with metal rings and are more durable than homemade ones.)

STUFFING: About $\frac{3}{4}$ oz. of polyester stuffing.

1. Trace and cut out the necessary pattern pieces.

For the Rabbit you will need to trace pattern pieces 1, 2, 9, 15, and 16 from Section VII. Cut patterns from sturdy paper or cardboard. Transfer all markings.

2. Trace around the patterns on the back of the fur.

You will need to draw:

Piece **1** (Body Back)—one right and one left

Piece **2** (Body Front)—one

Piece **9** (Head Back)—one right and one left

Piece **15** (Head Front)—one right and one left

Piece **16** (Ear)—two

3. Cut out the fur pieces.

Remember: Do not cut out the notches or the mouth line.

4. Cut out the velour pieces.

You will need to pin and cut out:

Piece **16** (Ear)—two (one pair for ear linings)

5. Zig-zag stitch the mouth lines on the head fronts, starting at A.

6. Pin and sew the head fronts together from B to C.

Remember: Be very careful to line up the mouths so that they come together exactly. Check the seam after you sew it, to make sure that the mouth is right.

7. Sew on a ball fringe nose at D.

8. Pin and sew the ears.

Pin one velour ear lining to each fur ear, right sides together. Match and pin the corners and the tip first. Have the velour side facing towards you when you pin and face down when you sew. This helps to keep the velour from rolling under and getting caught in the seam as you stitch.

Note: You must be particularly careful that the corners of the velour are not rolled under.

Trim the seam allowance at the tip of the ear, as indicated by the dotted lines on the pattern. Turn the ear right side out. Start at the point and push it through the ear, don't try to fold the

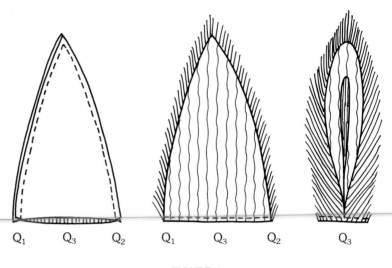

FIGURE 1

Q_1 Q_3 Q_2 Q_1 Q_3 Q_2 Q_3

open end back over the rest of the ear. A ball-point pen with the cap on makes a good tool to finish pushing the tip of the ear all the way out.

Pin and stitch the opening, $1/8''$ in from the edge. Fold both corners Q_1 and Q_2 in to the middle of the ear (Q_3) and pin. Sew across the end, $1/8''$ from the edge (see Figure 1).

9. Sew the ears to the head front.

Position one ear on each side of the center seam, as close to the seam as possible. Match the front of the ear (the side with the two edges folded in) to the pile side of the head front. Have the ears on top when you pin, and on the bottom when you sew. Stitch the ears $1/8''$ from the edge of the fabric (see Figure 2).

10. Insert the eyes.

11. Pin and sew the head backs together from B to G.

12. Pin and sew the head front to the head back from H to B to H.

Turn head right side out and set aside.

13. Pin and sew the body backs to the body front from J to K to L.

14. Trim the seam allowance at J and K, as indicated by the dotted lines on the pattern.

15. Pin and sew the head front to the body from M to C to M.

Remember: The head should be right side out and tucked down inside the body—which is still wrong side out—so that the pile sides of the fur are together.

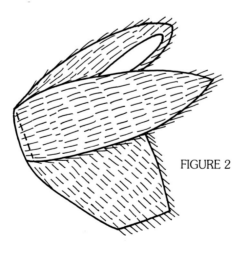

FIGURE 2

16. Turn the head wrong side out again.

17. Pin and sew the back seam from G to M to O.

18. Turn the puppet right side out.

Pull the ears down through the neck first. Then continue as you do with the other puppets.

19. Stuff the head.

20. Sew on the tail.

Position the tail at the center back seam, 1½″ above the lower edge of the puppet (this will make the edge of the pompon meet the lower edge of the puppet). Attach the pompon in the same way that you sew on a ball fringe nose.

21. Play with the puppet.

Lion

From the wilds of Africa comes this pride of lions. (Actually they're from the wilds of Missouri, but they like to pretend.)

Materials

BODY: Medium pile ($\frac{5}{16}''$–$\frac{1}{2}''$) blond, yellow, or gold fur.

MANE: Blond, yellow, or gold silky shag fur (about a one inch pile), that goes well with the body fur. Since it is harder to find the shag than it is to find the short fur, it is best to choose the shag first and then find the short fur to match it, rather than vice versa.

Note: Be extra careful when selecting the shag. Many shags are too stiff to use for puppets, or indeed for any stuffed animal. If you absolutely can't find any silky shags in the right color, you can use fantasy fur (craft fur).

NOSE: Small black ball fringe ($\frac{1}{2}''$).

EYES: 15 mm brown or orange crystal eyes.

STUFFING: About $\frac{3}{4}$ oz. of polyester stuffing.

1. Trace and cut out the necessary pattern pieces.

For the Lion you will need to trace pieces 1, 2, 10, 11, 12, 13, and 14 from Section VII. Cut patterns from sturdy paper or cardboard.

2. Trace around the pattern pieces on the back of the fur.

You will need to draw:

On the short fur:

Piece 1 (Body Back)—one right and one left

Piece 2 (Body Front)—one

Piece 10 (Ear)—four (two pairs)

Piece 11 (Head Front)—one right and one left

Piece 13 (Tail)—one

On the shag fur:

Piece 12 (Head Back)—one right and one left

Piece 14 (Tail Tip)—one

3. Cut out the fur pieces.

Remember: Do not cut out the notches or the mouth lines.

4. Zig-zag stitch the mouths on the head fronts, starting at A.

5. Pin and sew the head fronts together from B to C.

Remember: Line up the mouths exactly.

Because of the tight curves on the Lion's face, you will need to start at the neck and sew very slowly and carefully. After you have sewed and checked the seam, trim away half the seam allowance. Make sure that the notch for the nose is marked to the seam line, so that it won't be cut away completely when you trim the seam.

6. Sew on a ball-fringe nose at D.

7. Pin and sew the ears.

8. Sew the ears to the head front between notches E and F.

9. Insert the eyes.

10. Pin and sew the head backs together from B to G.

11. Pin and sew the head front to the head back from H to B to H. Turn the head right side out and set aside.

12. Pin and sew the body backs to the body front from J to K to L.

13. Trim the seam allowance at J and K, as indicated by the dotted lines on the pattern.

14. Pin and sew the head to the body from M to C to M.

Remember: The head should be right side out and tucked down inside the body, which is still wrong side out, so that the pile sides of the fur are facing.

15. Turn the head wrong side out again.

16. Assemble the tail.

Pin and sew the tail tip to the tail, matching P's (see Figure 1). Then, fold the tail in half lengthwise and sew from N to P to R (see Figure 2). Trim the seam allowance slightly at R. Turn the tail right side out, starting at the tip and poking it through the tail. (Don't try to start at the opening and turn it back over the tail.) Stuff the tail lightly, using small pieces of stuffing. Insert a pin parallel to the opening and about ⅝" from the opening, to hold the stuffing out of the way. Stitch across the opening, about ⅛" from the edge.

17. Pin and sew the tail to one body back, matching N's.

18. Pin and sew the back seam from G to M to O.

19. Turn the puppet right side out.

20. Stuff the head.

21. Play with the puppet.

Helpful Hint: Use recycled manila envelopes to keep your patterns for each animal puppet in order. On the outside of the envelope write the name of the puppet and also the numbers of the pattern pieces, so you can check before you start and make sure you have everything.

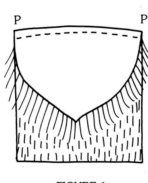

FIGURE 1

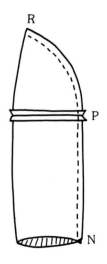

FIGURE 2

Cat

I hope you cat-lovers out there appreciate what I went through to design this simple little cat pattern. A realistic cat (as compared to a cartoon cat) is about the hardest animal to design that there is. I put in at least three times as much effort in designing this pattern as I did with any other pattern in the book, and the aggravation this cat caused me is immeasurable. These cats are all made from ⅜″ fur. Anything longer, and they start looking more like bears than cats. The cats look best in fur that is somewhat plush, rather than flat.

Materials

BODY: Short pile (³⁄₁₆″–¼″) to medium pile (⁵⁄₁₆″–⅜″) fur in any appropriate color.

WHISKERS: Black button-and-carpet thread.

NOSE: Small black ball fringe (½″).

EYES: 15 mm blue or brown crystal eyes. (Don't use the crystal cat eyes. They don't look right on a three-dimensional Cat. The Cat looks either cross-eyed or mean when you use cat eyes.)

STUFFING: About ¾ oz. of polyester stuffing.

1. Trace and cut out the necessary pattern pieces.

For the Cat you will need to trace pattern pieces 1, 2, 22, 23, 24, and 25 from Section VII. Cut patterns from sturdy paper or cardboard. Transfer all markings.

2. Trace around the patterns on the back of the fur.

For the Cat you will need to draw:

Piece 1 (Body Back)—one right and one left

Piece 2 (Body Front)—one

Piece 22 (Head Front)—one right and one left

Piece 23 (Ear)—two rights and two lefts

Piece 24 (Tail)—one

Piece 25 (Head Back)—one right and one left

3. Cut out the fur pieces.

Remember: Do not cut out the notches or the mouth lines.

4. Zig-zag stitch the mouth lines on the head fronts, starting at A.

On the Cat head, the left mouth line and the right mouth line form a sort of curved, inverted "V". Therefore, the zig-zag stitching should barely overlap

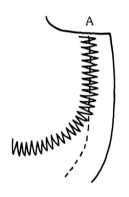

Wrong: too much overlap.

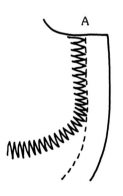

Wrong: too little overlap.

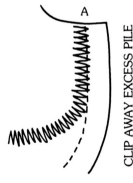

Right: just a bit of overlap.

CLIP AWAY EXCESS PILE

FIGURE 1

the seam line (see Figure 1). If you sew the zig-zag with the center of the zig-zag going down the ¼″ line, it will overlap too much, and will not show up well enough when the head is turned right side out. To compensate, you will need to shift the presser foot very slightly away from the edge, so that the zig-zag stitching overlaps the seam line very slightly. So that there won't be any pile sticking out where the inverted V comes together, clip the fur as indicated on the pattern *after* you have stitched the mouth lines, but *before* pinning and sewing the head fronts together.

5. Pin and sew the head fronts together from B to C.

After you sew the head fronts together, check to see if the mouth looks right. If it is not quite right, you may be able to correct it by re-stitching it. In the worst possible case you may have to rip out the seam and re-do it.

6. Sew on a ball fringe nose at D.

7. Pin and sew the ears.

Pin and sew the ears, leaving the bottom side open (the side that has slashes marked on it on the pattern). Trim the seam allowance to ⅛″. Turn the ears right side out. Sew across the opening ¼″ (*not* the usual ⅛″) from the edge. This is to staystitch the material and keep it from raveling when you slash it. Slash the edge from E to F, as indicated on the pattern (see Figure 2).

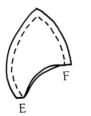 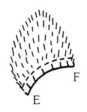

FIGURE 2

8. Pin and sew the ears to the head front between E and F.

Pin and stitch the ears in place (the slashes help you fit the curve of the ears to the opposite curve of the head). Sew ¼″ from the edge instead of the usual ⅛″. If you keep the ears facing towards you when you pin and down when you sew, it is easier to see what you are doing. However, if you do the reverse, and have the head front facing towards you when you pin and down when you sew, it is easier to keep the ear pleated a bit, so that the edge is straight as you stitch. Take your pick.

9. Insert the eyes.

10. Make the whiskers.

Using a double strand of black button-and-carpet thread, take a stitch at the dot at letter P, starting from the pile side through the fabric and back out the pile side (if you have trouble finding the dot from the pile side, push a pin through P from the fabric side). Leave a "tail" of thread hanging on the pile side, about 3″ long. Take another stitch in the same place, and this time pull the stitch tight. Cut your thread, again leaving a tail about 3″ long. If you have done this right, you should then have four "whiskers", with a tight stitch between them. Repeat for the other side of the face.

11. Pin and sew the head backs together from B to G.

12. Pin and sew the head front to the head back from H to B to H.

Make sure you keep the whiskers out of the way of the seam. Turn the head right side out and set aside.

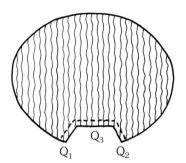

FIGURE 2

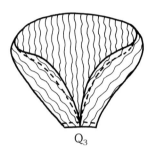

FIGURE 3

the ears right side out. Sew the opening shut ⅛″ from the edge (see Figure 2). Fold both corners of the ear in to the center, as indicated on the pattern (see Figure 3). Pin and sew across the bottom edge, again ⅛″ from the edge.

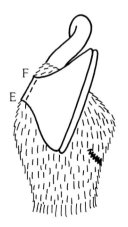

FIGURE 4

9. Sew the ears to the head front between notches E and F (see Figure 4).

10. Insert the eyes.

11. Pin and sew the head backs together from B to G.

12. Pin and sew the head front to the head back from H to B to H. Turn head right side out and set aside.

13. Pin and sew the body backs to the body front from J to K to L.

14. Trim the seam allowance at J and K, as indicated by the dotted lines on the pattern.

15. Pin and sew the head to the body from M to C to M.

Remember that the head is right side out and tucked inside the body, which is still wrong side out, so that the pile sides of the fur are facing.

16. Turn the head wrong side out again.

17. Make the yarn tail.

Cut the yarn about 12″ long (longer if you prefer an extra-long tail). For fingering yarn you will need 24 pieces. For worsted weight yarn you will need 9 to 12 pieces, depending on whether you want the tail to be thick or thin. Knot the pieces together at one end.

18. Pin and sew the tail to one body back.

Position the tail at notch N. With the right side of the body facing you, lay the tail down on the fur with the knot extending over the edge of the fabric (so that you won't have to sew through the knot). Make sure that you have the tail on the pile side and the knot at the edge (see Figure 5).

19. Pin and sew the back seam from G to M to O.

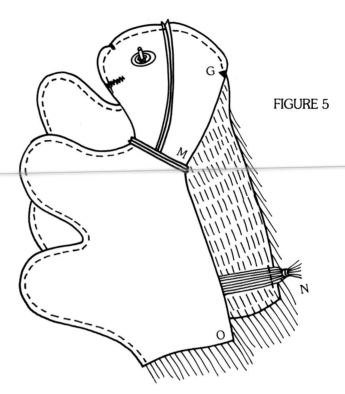

FIGURE 5

20. Turn the puppet right side out.

Pull the ears down through the neck opening first, then proceed in the usual way.

21. Stuff the head.

22. Braid the tail.

Divide the strands of yarn into three equal sections. Holding the puppet between your knees so that you can keep the yarn taut, braid the tail to as close to the end of the yarn as possible. With thread to match the yarn, stitch back and forth across the end of the braid, about 1″ from the end of the yarn strands. Unbraid the ends that are be-low the stitching and trim the ends evenly, either close to the stitching, or ½″ past the stitching, depending on your preference.

23. Play with the puppet.

Helpful Hint: Don't waste anything. Sort your scraps and any that are ab-solutely too little to make even a finger puppet out of can be given to nursery schools, day care centers, kindergar-tens, and elementary school art teach-ers. The littlest kids like to feel the furry scraps and the older kids can make amusing animal pictures by gluing pieces of fur onto construction paper.

Dog

Although these pups were not free, their upkeep is minimal—no shots, no vet bills, and they don't eat enough to make a bit of difference. They are always ready to play, they never bite, and they are guaranteed housebroken. They don't have a pedigree, but with the right sort of fur you could make a cocker spaniel or even a poodle.

Materials

BODY: Short pile ($\frac{3}{16}''$–$\frac{1}{4}''$) to medium pile ($\frac{5}{16}''$–$\frac{1}{2}''$) fur in any appropriate color (brown, black, tan, rust, white, spotted, etc.). The Dog looks especially nice in Persian lamb type fur and other irregular pile furs.

EARS: Velour that coordinates with the fur.

NOSE: Small black ball fringe ($\frac{1}{2}''$).

EYES: 15 mm brown or blue crystal eyes.

STUFFING: About $\frac{3}{4}$ oz. of polyester stuffing.

1. Trace and cut out the necessary pattern pieces.

For the Dog you will need to trace pattern pieces 1, 2, 9, 19, 20, and 21 from Section VII. Cut patterns from sturdy paper or cardboard. Transfer all markings.

2. Draw around the pattern on the back of the fur.

For the Dog you will need to draw:

Piece 1 (Body Back)—one right and one left

Piece 2 (Body Front)—one

Piece 9 (Head Back)—one right and one left

Piece 19 (Head Front)—one right and one left

Piece 20 (Tail)—one

Piece 21 (Ear)—one right and one left

Remember: to mark dark fur you will need to use white ball-point fabric paint.

3. Cut out the fur pieces.

Remember: Do not cut out the notches or the mouth lines.

4. Cut out the velour pieces.

You will need to pin and cut out:

Piece 21 (Ear)—one right and one left (one pair)

5. Zig-zag stitch the mouth lines on the head fronts, starting at A.

6. Pin and sew the head fronts together from B to C.

Remember to be extra careful when you match up the mouths, and check the point where they meet, after you sew the seam. Trim seam to $\frac{1}{8}''$, as indicated by the dotted lines on the pattern.

7. Sew on a ball fringe nose at D.

8. Pin and sew the ears to the ear linings.

Have the velour facing towards you when you pin and down when you sew. Trim the seam, turn the ears right side out, and sew across the opening, $\frac{1}{8}''$ in from the edges.

9. Sew the ears to the head front between notches E and F.

Since the ears are not symmetrical, make sure that point E on the ear is matched with notch E on the head front; ditto the F's. Pin and stitch the velour side of the ear next to the pile side of the head front.

10. Insert the eyes.

11. Pin and sew the head backs together from B to G.

12. Pin and sew the head front to the head back from H to B to H. Turn head right side out and set aside.

13. Pin and sew the body backs to the body front from J to K to L.

14. Trim the seam allowance at J and K, as indicated by the dotted lines on the pattern.

15. Pin and sew the head to the body from M to C to M.

Don't forget that the head is still right side out and tucked down inside the body (which is wrong side out), so that the pile sides of the fur are facing.

16. Turn the head wrong side out again.

17. Pin, sew, and stuff the tail.

Fold tail in half and stitch as indicated on pattern. Trim seam ⅛″. Turn, and stuff.

18. Pin and sew the tail to one body back, matching N's.

19. Pin and sew the back seam from G to M to O.

20. Turn the puppet right side out.

Pull the ears down through the neck opening first, then proceed in the usual way to turn the puppet right side out.

21. Stuff the head.

Sometimes, if the fur is stiff, the Dog's ears stick out from his head like wings. Usually, holding the ears down for awhile is enough to make the ears hang down properly, but if that doesn't work, you may need to tack the ears down.

22. Play with the puppet.

Helpful Hint: When cutting out a puppet that is drawn on a large piece of fur, it is sometimes awkward to handle such a heavy piece of fur. For this reason, it helps to cut along the lines that separate the puppet from the rest of the fur first, so that you will have a smaller piece of fur to manipulate when you begin to cut out the individual pattern pieces.

III. NEW FACES: DIFFERENT HEAD CONSTRUCTIONS

Possum

This is the American possum, not to be confused with the Australian possum, which is a totally different animal. The possum is the only marsupial native to North America, and its extreme stupidity makes it an easy prey to automobiles.

Materials

BODY BACK: Shag fur (1½"–2") in a Possum color (beige, gray, beige/black, etc.). If you can't find any nice shags that look like a Possum, you can use fantasy fur (also called craft fur) that is available in most craft shops and discount stores.

BODY FRONT: Light-colored velour, in beige, tan, gray, etc., that coordinates well with the fur.

EARS: Dark velour, such as black or dark brown, that coordinates well with both the fur and the light velour.

TAIL: Yarn that goes well with the fur and velour, preferably light-colored. (You may think that it is hard to find three different kinds of fabric, plus yarn, which go together well. You are right. But, it *can* be done!)

NOSE: Small black ball fringe (½").

EYES: 15 mm brown crystal eyes (or you may prefer blue eyes for a gray Possum).

STUFFING: About ¾ oz. of polyester stuffing.

1. Trace and cut out the necessary pattern pieces.

For the Possum you will need to trace pattern pieces 1, 26, 27, 28, and 29 from Section VII. Cut pattern pieces from sturdy paper or cardboard. Transfer all markings.

2. Trace around the pattern on the back of the fur.

For the Possum you will need to draw:

Piece 1 (Body Back)—one right and one left

Piece 27 (Head Back)—one right and one left

3. Cut out the fur pieces.

4. Cut out the velour pieces.

You will need to pin, cut out, and mark:

From the dark velour:

Piece 29 (Ear)—four (two pairs)

From the light velour:

Piece 26 (Body Front)—one

Piece 28 (Head Front)—one right and one left (one pair)

When cutting velour double, remember to put the right sides together so the pattern pieces will slip less. After cutting the head fronts and body front, use the pattern as a stencil and mark the notches, the mouth, and the eye position with a pen, as you do when marking the head fronts on fur fabric. *Do not* cut out notches of mouth lines.

5. Zig-zag the mouth on the head fronts starting at A.

You may have trouble with the edges of the velour slipping down inside the feed plate when you try to stitch it. There are three things you can do to help prevent this. (1) Use a smaller needle than you use for the fur. (2) Hold the fabric stretched tight when you sew. (3) Just backstitch with the straight stitch when you start. In other words, don't stitch forward, then back, then forward with the zig-zag. Start a little past the beginning (point A), stitch backwards to the beginning with a straight stitch, and then stitch forward with the zig-zag. Whatever you do, don't start sewing at the edge of the

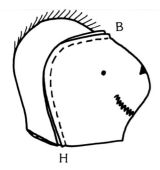

FIGURE 1

and then sewing them together (see Figure 1). This differs from the puppets in Sections I and II for which you construct a *front* head and a *back* head and sew them together.

Be careful to match the correct edge of each head back to the proper head front. If it seems easy to match the curves to each other, you probably have the wrong edge of the head back—the correct edge of the head back is not easy to match to the head front. Because of the different curves on the head front and head back, it is easier to sew them if you hold the head front facing towards you when you pin and face down when you sew.

Note: This is just the opposite from the way you pin most of the puppet heads.

10. Pin and sew the right half of the head to the left half from G to B to C.

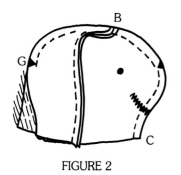

FIGURE 2

You will need to use matching thread when you sew, because the seam will show when you sew corduroy. Also, be very careful to line up the mouths exactly. Any discrepancy will show up even more on the corduroy than it would on the fur (see Figure 2).

11. Sew on a ball fringe nose at D.

12. Insert the eyes.

Turn the head right side out and set aside.

13. Sew the hem on the body front.

Since the body front of the Hedgehog is made of fabric, it needs to be hemmed across the bottom to give it a nice edge. Fold up a narrow (¼″) double hem and stitch across it from L to L.

14. Pin and sew the body backs to the body front from J to K to L.

It is always best to work with the corduroy facing towards you when you pin and down when you sew. This helps keep the corduroy from rolling over and getting caught in the seam. For this reason, ignore my usual rule about having the neck to your right when you pin. Instead, keep the corduroy facing towards you when you pin and down when you stitch.

15. Trim the seam allowance at J and K, as indicated by the dotted lines on the pattern.

16. Pin and sew the head to the body from M to C to M.

As always, the head should be right side out and tucked down inside the body, which is still wrong side out.

17. Turn the head wrong side out again.

18. Pin and sew the back seam from G to M to O.

19. Turn the puppet right side out.

20. Stuff the head.

You will find that it is harder to stuff a corduroy head smoothly than it is to stuff a fur head. The fur hides small irregularities and the fabric doesn't.

21. Play with the puppet.

A real hedgehog can curl up in a ball with only his prickles showing. You can make your Hedgehog Puppet curl up in a ball too!

Helpful Hint: Use clear plastic bags to avoid losing little pieces of cut out puppets. Put all the pieces for one puppet in one bag. The bags can be used over and over again, and the clear plastic lets you see exactly what each bag contains.

Monkey

These monkeys remind me of some four-year-old boys I have known. The smiles and the mischief are the same with both the boys and the monkeys, but only the monkeys have curly tails.

It is fun to pick the fur for the monkeys, since there are so many possibilities. Because the face is velour, you can get away with using slightly longer fur for the monkey than you can use for most of the other puppets.

When choosing fur for the monkeys, you can make the fur a light color and the velour dark, or the fur dark and the velour light. You can use fur and velour that are two shades of the same color, like gray. You can use two different, but closely related colors, like rust fur and bright gold velour. Just let your imagination run wild!

Materials:

BODY: Medium pile ($\frac{5}{16}''$–$\frac{1}{2}''$) fur in any shade of beige, brown, rust, tan, or gray.

FACE AND EARS: Velour that is lighter or darker than the fur, but which blends well with it. There should be merely a slight contrast between the fur and the velour.

NOSE: Small black ball fringe ($\frac{1}{2}''$).

EYES: 15 mm brown crystal eyes. Some people may prefer the smaller 12 mm size. When inserting the eyes, you can try different sizes before locking them into place.

STUFFING: About $\frac{3}{4}$ oz. of polyester stuffing.

1. Trace and cut out the necessary pattern pieces.

For the Monkey you will need to trace pattern pieces 1, 2, 27, 33, 34, 35, and 36 from Section VII. Cut patterns from sturdy paper or cardboard.

2. Trace around the patterns on the back of the fur.

You will need to draw:

Piece 1 (Body Back)—one right and one left

Piece 2 (Body Front)—one

Piece 27 (Head Back)—one right and one left

Piece 34 (Lower Face)—one right and one left

Piece 36 (Tail)—one

3. Cut out the fur pieces.

Remember: Don't cut out the notches.

4. Cut out the velour pieces.

You will need to pin, cut out, and mark:

Piece 33 (Upper Face)—one left and one right (one pair)

Piece 35 (Ear)—two lefts and two rights (two pairs)

Working with the velour folded double (right sides together), you will cut out piece 33 once and piece 35 twice. Don't forget that velour has a nap, so the material should be folded lengthwise, not crosswise. Also, be sure the arrows on all pattern pieces are lined up in the same direction. After cutting the upper faces, use the pattern as a stencil, and with a pen mark the notches, the eye dot, and the mouth lines. *Do not cut the notches or the mouth lines.*

5. Zig-zag stitch the mouth lines on the head fronts, starting at A.

You may have trouble with the edge of the velour slipping down inside the feed plate of the machine when you try to stitch on it. There are three things you can do to help prevent this. (1) Use a smaller needle than you use for the fur. (2) Hold the fabric stretched tight when you sew. (3) Just backstitch with the straight stitch when you start. Don't stitch forward, then back, then forward with the zig-zag—just start a little past the beginning point, stitch backwards to the beginning with a straight stitch, and *then* stitch forward with the zig-zag. Whatever you do, don't start sewing at the edge of the fabric instead of at A—that is almost guaranteed to jam the velour down inside your machine.

7. With fur sides together, pin and sew the ear fronts (white fur) to the ear backs (body color fur).

After sewing, trim the seam, turn the ears right side out and sew across the opening ⅛″ from the edge, as usual.

8. Pin and sew the ears to the head front from F to E.

Make sure that the front ear (with the white fur) is against the pile side of the head front when you pin.

9. Insert the eyes.

10. Sew on a ball fringe nose.

11. Sew the head backs together from B to G.

12. Sew the head fronts to the head backs from H to E to F to B to F to E to H.

Turn head right side out and set aside.

13. Pin and sew the body backs to the body front from J to K to L.

14. Trim the seam allowance at J and K, as indicated by the dotted lines on the pattern.

15. Pin and sew the head to the body from M to C to M.

Don't forget that the head is right side out and tucked down inside the body, which is wrong side out. Because of its width the head may be more difficult to sew to the body than earlier puppet heads were.

16. Turn the head wrong side out again.

17. Pin and sew the back seam from G to M to O.

18. Turn the puppet right side out.

19. Stuff the head.

20. Play with the puppet.

Raccoon

Although the Germans call the raccoon a Waschbaer (wash-bear), raccoons are more closely related to pandas than they are to regular bears. The relationship is quite obvious to me—you have to appliqué black eye patches on each of them!

Materials

BODY: Medium pile ($\frac{5}{16}''$–$\frac{1}{2}''$) fur in medium to medium-dark brown.

TAIL AND EYE PATCHES: Medium pile ($\frac{5}{16}''$–$\frac{1}{2}''$) black fur.

LOWER HEAD FRONT: Medium pile ($\frac{5}{16}''$–$\frac{1}{2}''$) white fur.

Note: It is important that all three colors of fur are the same length and density. This is not easy to find, unfortunately. The most important thing is to make sure that the brown and black furs are the same length so that the tail doesn't look like link sausages.

EAR LININGS: Velour the same color as the body, or as close in color as you can find. If you absolutely can't find any velour that looks good with the fur, you can make the ear linings from fur, but the velour looks a little nicer.

NOSE: Small black ball fringe ($\frac{1}{2}''$).

EYES: 15 mm brown crystal eyes.

STUFFING: About $\frac{3}{4}$ oz. of polyester stuffing.

1. Trace and cut out the necessary pattern pieces.

For the Raccoon you will need to trace pattern pieces 1, 2, 37, 38, 39, 40, 41, 42, 43, 44, 45, and 46 from Section VII. This sounds like a lot of pieces, but most of the extra pieces are for the stripes in the tail. Cut patterns from sturdy paper or cardboard. Transfer all markings.

2. Draw around the patterns on the back of the fur.

You will need to draw:

On the brown fur:

Piece 1 (Body Back)—one right and one left

Piece 2 (Body Front)—one

Piece 37 (Ear)—two

Piece 40 (Second Tail Stripe)—one

Piece 42 (Fourth Tail Stripe)—one

Piece 44 (Head Back)—one right and one left

Piece 46 (Upper Head Front)—one right and one left

On the black fur:

Piece 38 (Eye Patch)—one right and one left

Piece 39 (First Tail Stripe)—one

Piece 41 (Third Tail Stripe)—one

Piece 43 ((Fifth Tail Stripe)—one

On the white fur:

Piece 45 (Lower Head Front)—one right and one left

Note: Because the large number of pieces can get very confusing, it is a good idea to sort them all out before you start tracing them onto the fur. Put all the ones for the brown fur in one pile, all the ones for the black fur in a different pile, and set the one for the white fur aside by itself. Otherwise, you may end up with a lot of pieces cut out of the wrong color fur.

3. Cut out the fur pieces.

Remember: Do not cut out the notches or the mouth lines.

4. Cut out the velour pieces.

IV. TAILS, SCALES, AND OTHER BODY DESIGNS

Fox

For a slim, sleek-looking fox, use ³⁄₁₆″ fur. For a slightly fatter fox, use ⁵⁄₁₆″ fur and for a long-haired fox, use ⁹⁄₁₆″ fur. Try making foxes in all three types of fur—you'll be surprised at how different they look.

Materials

BODY: Short pile (³⁄₁₆″–¼″) to medium pile (⁵⁄₁₆″–½″) rust fur.

CHEST, LOWER HEAD FRONT, TAIL TIP: Short pile (³⁄₁₆″–¼″) to medium pile (⁵⁄₁₆″–½″) white fur.

OPTIONAL: Make the tail of rust fantasy fur (also called craft fur), and the tail-tip of white fantasy fur. This is especially nice to do when the body fur is short—the tail doesn't look really great in short fur.

EAR LININGS: White velour.

NOSE: Small black ball fringe (½″).

EYES: 15 mm orange or brown crystal eyes. (The orange looks better with the rust fur, but if you don't have orange, you can use brown.)

STUFFING: About ¾ oz. of polyester stuffing.

1. Trace and cut out the necessary pattern pieces.

For the Fox you will need to trace pattern pieces 1, 47, 48, 49, 50, 51, 52, 53, 54, and 55 from Section VII. Cut patterns from sturdy paper or cardboard. Transfer all markings.

2. Trace around the patterns on the back of the fur.

You will need to draw:

On the rust fur:

Piece 1 (Body Back)—one right and one left

Piece 49 (Upper Head Front)—one right and one left

Piece 50 (Legs Front)—one right and one left

Piece 52 (Ear)—one right and one left

Piece 54 (Tail)—two (optional—cut this of rust fantasy fur)

Piece 55 (Head Back)—one right and one left

On the white fur:

Piece 47 (Tail Tip)—two (optional—cut this of white fantasy fur)

Piece 48 (Lower Head Front)—one right and one left

Piece 51 (Chest)—one

3. Cut out the fur pieces.

Remember: Do not cut the notches or the mouth lines.

4. Cut out the velour pieces.

You will need to pin and cut out:

Piece 53 (Ear Lining)—one right and one left (one pair)

5. Zig-zag stitch the mouth lines on the right and left lower head fronts, starting at A.

6. Pin and sew the upper head fronts to the lower head fronts from U to T to S (see Figure 1).

Be careful that you don't get the upper head front upside down, because when it is right side up, it looks upside down!

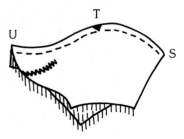

FIGURE 1

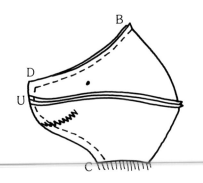

FIGURE 2

7. Pin and sew the head fronts together from B to U to C.

After sewing this seam, trim the seam allowance a bit at the nose but don't lose track of notch D, indicating where to sew the ball fringe nose (see Figure 2).

8. Sew on a ball fringe nose at D.

9. Pin and sew the ears.

Since the ear lining is smaller than the ear, hold the lining facing towards you as you pin. Put in a pin at W first, (see Figure 3) then E, then X, then insert the pins along the seam lines in between. Have the velour side face down on the machine when you sew, and that way you can hold the extra fur ear material out of the way as you stitch. Trim the seam allowance at the tip of each ear and turn the ears right side

out (see Figure 4). Fold the ear along the fold line at F, as indicated on the pattern. The open edges at the base of the ear should now match. Stay-stitch across the opening $\frac{1}{4}''$ from the edge (*not* the usual $\frac{1}{8}''$). Slash the seam allowance. This allows you to stretch the edge of the ear to match the curve of the head front (see Figure 5).

10. Pin and sew the ears to the head front between notches E and F.

Make sure that the velour side of the ear is next to the pile side of the face when you pin. Since there is a left ear and a right ear, be sure to match up the letters on the pattern pieces.

You may either work with the fur side of the face towards you as you pin, so that it will be face down when you sew and you can see what you are doing, or, you can have the fabric side of the face towards you when you pin, so the ear is up when you sew, enabling you to "pleat" the ear better, so that the curve of the ear straightens out and matches the curve of the face. Use whichever method feels most comfortable.

11. Insert the eyes.

12. Pin and sew the head backs together from B to G.

13. Pin and sew the head back to the head front from H to B to H. Turn head right side out and set aside.

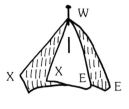

FIGURE 3

FIGURE 4

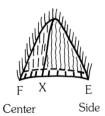

Center   Side

FIGURE 5

76

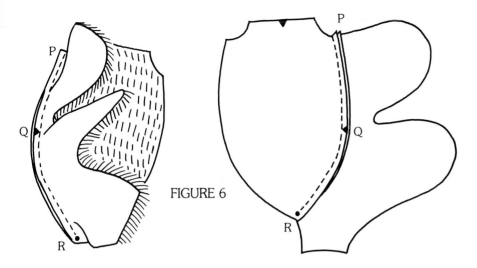

FIGURE 6

14. Pin and sew the chest to the right and left front leg pieces from P to Q to R.

Pin and sew one pair of legs to the chest first. Have the chest towards you when you pin, and face down on the machine when you sew.

Note: Do not sew all the way to the edge of the fur at R. Stop at the dot— ¼" from the edge of the fabric (see Figure 6).

Pin and sew the second pair of legs to the chest, the same way as the first pair, again ending the seam at the dot.

15. Pin and sew the front legs together from S to R.

Again, end the seam at the dot at R (see Figure 7).

16. Pin and sew the body backs to the body front from J to K to L.

Ignore the rule about having the neck

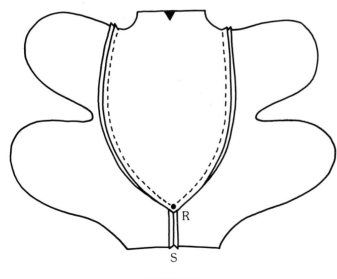

FIGURE 7

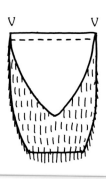

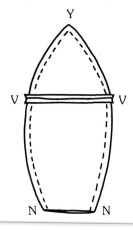

FIGURE 8   FIGURE 9

to the right when you pin. Instead, have the body backs towards you when you pin. That way you can maneuver past the seams on the front more easily.

17. Trim the seam allowance at J and K, as indicated by the dotted lines on the pattern.

18. Pin and sew the head to the body from M to C to M.

Don't forget to have the head right side out and tucked down inside the body, which is still wrong side out.

19. Turn the head wrong side out again.

20. Pin and sew the tail.

Sew the tail tips to the tails, matching V's (see Figure 8). Pin and sew the tails together from N to V to Y to V to N (see Figure 9). Turn the tail right side out and stuff it lightly. (A ball-point pen with the cap on makes a good tool for stuffing the tail.) Stitch across the bottom of the tail from N to N, ⅛″ in from the edges.

21. Pin and sew the tail to one body back, matching one N on the tail seam with the N on the body back.

22. Pin and sew the back seam from G to M to O.

23. Turn the puppet right side out.

24. Stuff the head.

25. Play with the puppet.

Dragon

The dragon is your chance to release your inhibitions! Instead of staid brown bears, and ordinary gray mice, and plain gold lions, you can live it up with blue-striped dragons, dragons with plaid tummys, purple dragons with pink polka-dots (assuming you can find the fur!). The only problem I have with making dragons is deciding which of the many possible combinations to make!

Materials

BODY: Short pile (³⁄₁₆″–¼″) to medium pile (⁵⁄₁₆″–½″) fur in fanciful colors— blues, reds, oranges, greens, purples, pinks, plaids, stripes, etc.

CHEST, LOWER HEAD FRONT: Short pile (³⁄₁₆″–¼″) to medium pile (⁵⁄₁₆″–½″) fur in a different color from the body fur. It is better to have the two colors closely related on the color wheel, rather than far apart (i.e., green with yellow or blue, red with pink, orange, or purple, blue with green or purple, etc.) It also looks best if the chest fur is a lighter color than the body fur, since animals usually have a lighter underbody. *Note:* The chest fur should be the same length or shorter than the body fur. It should *not* be longer than the body fur.

BUMPS: Velour to match the chest fur color, or in a third complementary color.

EYES: 15 mm crystal eyes in any color that looks good with the fur you have picked.

STUFFING: About ¾ oz. of polyester stuffing.

1. Trace and cut out the necessary pattern pieces.

For the Dragon you will need to trace pattern pieces 1, 50, 51, 56, 57, 58, 59, 60, and 61 from Section VII. Cut patterns from sturdy paper or cardboard. Transfer all markings.

Note: On pattern piece 61, cut out the dart P-P, so that you can use the paper pattern as a stencil for marking the stitching line on the back of the fur. However, *do not* cut out the dart on the fur.

2. Trace around the patterns on the back of the fur.

You will need to draw:

On the main color fur:

Piece 1 (Body Back)—one right and one left

Piece 50 (Leg Front)—one right and one left

Piece 58 (Head Back)—one right and one left

Piece 59 (Tail)—one right and one left

Piece 61 (Upper Head Front)—one (mark the dart P-P, but *do not* cut it out).

On the contrasting color fur:

Piece 51 (Chest)—one

Piece 60 (Lower Head Front)—one

3. Cut out the fur pieces.

Remember: Do *not* cut out the notches or the eyebrow lines.

4. Cut out the velour pieces.

You will need to pin, cut out, and mark:

Piece 56 (Tail Bumps)—one left and one right (one pair)

Piece 57 (Head Bumps)—one left and one right (one pair)

Remember: The velour has a nap, so pin and cut out the pattern pieces accordingly. After cutting out the velour pieces, use a pen to mark the notches on the right side of the velour, since

this is the side that you will be able to see when you are matching head and tail bump notches with the Dragon head and tail.

5. Zig-zag stitch the eyebrows on the upper head front, starting at the A's.

6. Sew the dart in the middle of the upper head front from P to P.

If you have marked the fabric side of the fur properly, this will be an easy dart to sew. Fold the dart so that a P is at each end, and follow the stitching line marked on the fabric. You don't need to trim or clip the dart.

7. Sew the nose dart Q to R.

Match the corners Q and sew from Q to R.

8. Sew the lower head front to the upper head front from E to F to Q to F to E (see Figure 1).

Have the upper head front facing towards you when you pin and face down on the machine when you sew.

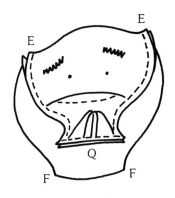

FIGURE 1

9. Insert the eyes.

After you have gotten this far, turn the head front right side out and admire it while you struggle with the dragon bumps.

10. Sew the dragon bumps.

Pin the right and left sides of each pair of dragon bumps together, right sides facing. Check the patterns to see how the stitching line goes. Sew, trying desperately to keep the velour from slipping. I haven't found any really good way to keep it from slipping, except sheer determination and lots of pins. (Lots of pins = one pin at each end, one at each "peak" and one in each "valley".) Not expecting perfection also helps!

Trim the seam allowance to 1/8" and turn the bumps right side out. (Make sure you can see the notches at G and V when the bumps are right side out. Mark them again if necessary.) Sew across the bottom opening on each set of bumps 1/4" from the edge. Clip the seam allowance to the stitching line, as indicated on the pattern. This will enable you to match the curve on the bumps to the curves on the head back and tail.

11. Sew the bumps to the head and tail.

An easy way to tell the head bumps from the tail bumps is that the head has four bumps and the tail has three. Pin the head bumps to one head back

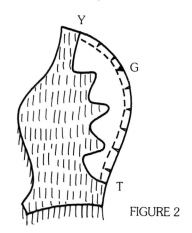

FIGURE 2

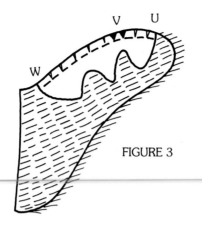

FIGURE 3

12. Pin and sew the head back from B to G.

13. Pin and sew the head front to the head back from H to B to H.

Have the head front towards you when you pin and down when you sew. Turn the head right side out and set aside.

14. Pin and sew the chest to the left and right leg fronts from P to Q to dot at R.

Pin and sew one pair of legs to the chest first, having the chest towards you when you pin. Sew with the chest face down on the machine, starting at P and ending at the dot at R (stop stitching *exactly* at dot R), ¼″ in from the edge of the fabric (see Figure 4). Sew the other pair of legs to the chest in the same way, again ending the seam at the dot R.

15. Pin and sew the leg fronts together from S to R.

Again, stitch and end the seam at the dot at R (see Figure 5).

16. Pin and sew the body backs to the body front from J to K to L.

between T and Y, matching notches G (see Figure 2). Make sure that the bumps are positioned on the fur side of the head back. Have the head back facing towards you when you pin and face down when you sew. Sew the bumps ¼″ from the edge.

Next, pin the tail bumps to one tail piece, between the notches U and W, matching double notches V (see Figure 3). Again, have the body piece facing towards you when you pin and down when you sew, and sew ¼″ from the edge.

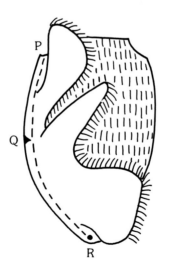

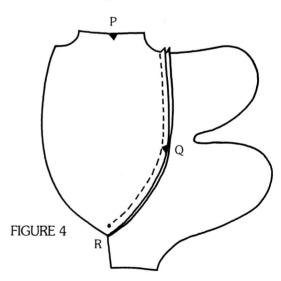

FIGURE 4

82

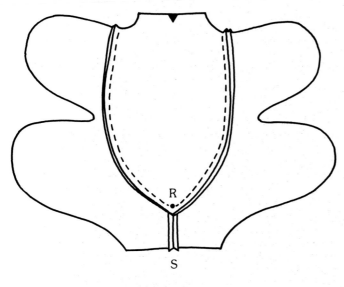

FIGURE 5

Instead of having the neck to the right when you pin, have the body back towards you when you pin and face down when you sew. This makes it easier to maneuver past the seams on the body front.

17. Pin and sew the head to the body from M to C to M.

Remember: Have the head right side out and tucked down inside the body (which is still wrong side out).

18. Turn the head wrong side out again.

19. Pin and sew the tail from X to W to V to U to N (see Figure 6).

After sewing the tail, turn it right side out and stuff it very softly. Use a pin to keep the stuffing away from the opening. Stitch across the opening from X to N, 1/8" from the raw edges.

20. Pin and sew the tail to one body back, matching N's.

21. Pin and sew the back seam from G to M to O.

22. Turn the puppet right side out.

23. Stuff the head.

24. Play with the puppet.

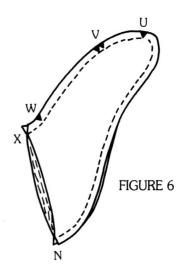

FIGURE 6

Alligator

It is very hard to distinguish alligators from crocodiles. To be perfectly honest, I'm not sure if these are alligators or crocodiles. I have assumed that they are alligators, because alligators very seldom eat people, and this one hasn't eaten anyone yet.

Materials

BODY: Short pile (³⁄₁₆″–¼″) to medium pile (⁵⁄₁₆″–½″) fur in any shade of green.

TUMMY, LOWER HEAD FRONT: Short pile (³⁄₁₆″–¼″) to medium pile (⁵⁄₁₆″–½″) fur in a lighter shade of green than the body. If two shades of green are not available, you can use yellow for the tummy. Make sure that the tummy fur is not longer than the body fur.

EYES: 15 mm crystal eyes, either blue, brown, or orange, whichever you prefer.

STUFFING: About ¾ oz. of polyester stuffing.

1. Trace and cut out the necessary pattern pieces.

For the Alligator you will need to trace pattern pieces 1, 58, 59, 60, 61, 62, and 63 from Section VII. Cut patterns from sturdy paper or cardboard. Transfer all markings.

Note: On pattern piece 61, cut out the dart P-P, so that you can use the pattern as a stencil and mark the stitching line on the back of the fur. *Don't* cut the dart out of the fur, however.

2. Trace around the pattern pieces on the back of the fur.

You will need to draw:

On the dark fur:

Piece 1 (Body Back)—one right and one left

Piece 58 (Head Back)—one right and one left

Piece 59 (Tail)—one right and one left

Piece 61 (Upper Head Front)—one (mark the dart P-P with a pen)

Piece 63 (Leg Front)—one right and one left

On the light fur:

Piece 60 (Lower Head Front)—one

Piece 62 (Tummy)—one

3. Cut out the fur pieces.

Remember: Do not cut the notches or the eyebrow lines.

4. Zig-zag stitch the eyebrows on the upper head front, starting at A.

5. Sew the dart in the middle of the upper head front, from P to P.

If you have marked the fabric side of the fur properly, this will be an easy dart to sew. Fold the dart so that a P is at each end, and follow the stitching line marked on the fabric. (You don't need to trim or clip the dart.)

6. Sew the nose dart Q to R.

Match the corners Q and sew from Q to R.

7. Pin and sew the lower head front to the upper head front from E to F to Q to F to E.

Have the lower head front towards you when you pin and face down on the machine when you sew. That way you can maneuver around the darts without catching too much of the upper head front in the seam.

8. Insert the eyes.

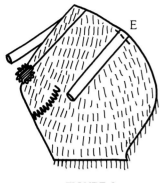

FIGURE 2

direction when the head is done (see Figure 2). This is one of those things that is easier said than done. Actually, close to perpendicular is good enough.

10. Insert the eyes.

11. Pin and sew the right and left head backs together from B to G.

12. Pin and sew the head back to the head front from H to B to H. Turn head right side out and set aside.

13. Appliqué the spots to the body back.

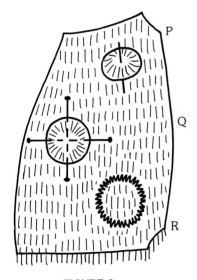

FIGURE 3

If you have already made a Raccoon or a Panda, you will know what you have in store for you.

Brush all the pile to the center of one of the spots. Stick a pin up through one of the dots on the body back that shows where a spot should be. Then stick the pin through the dot in the center of the spot (the fabric side of the spot should be against the fur side of the body back). Hold the spot and the body back together while you pin them (see Figure 3). If the center pin sticks out crooked, shift the spot slightly, so that the center pin comes straight out of the fabric. After you have pinned around the edge of the spot, remove the center pin. Using a stitch width of about half the maximum zig-zag, and a stitch length slightly longer than you use to zig-zag the mouths, sew around the edge of the spot. Stop frequently and use a pin to tuck the pile under the presser foot.

When you finish the first spot, admire how nice it looks, and try not to think about the five other spots you still have to do.

Repeat the procedure for the remaining five spots.

14. Pin and sew the leg backs to the body backs from P to Q to R.

Have the body backs facing towards you when you pin, and face down when you sew.

15. Pin and sew the body backs to the body front from J to K to L.

Instead of having the neck to your right when you pin, have the body front facing towards you when you pin and face down when you sew. This makes it easier to maneuver around the narrow seam point at K.

16. Trim the seam allowance at J and K, as indicated by the dotted lines on the pattern.

17. Pin and sew the head to the body from M to C to M.

The head should be right side out and tucked down inside of the body, which is still wrong side out.

18. Turn the head wrong side out again.

19. Pin and sew the back seam from G to M to O.

20. Turn the puppet right side out.

21. Stuff the head.

22. Play with the puppet.

Panda

91

If you ever get a chance to see the pandas in the Washington Zoo, do so. It is so neat—they look just like stuffed animals!

Materials

BODY: Short pile ($3/16''$–$1/4''$) to medium pile ($5/16''$–$1/2''$) fur in both white and black. Plush fur looks best, but it is often hard to find plush white fur. The most important thing is to have both colors of fur the same length and density.

NOSE: Small black ball fringe ($1/2''$).

EYES: 15 mm blue crystal eyes.

STUFFING: About $3/4$ oz. of polyester stuffing.

1. Trace and cut out the necessary pattern pieces.

For the Panda you will need to trace pattern pieces 10, 64, 65, 66, 67, 68, 69, 70, 71, and 72 from Section VII. Cut patterns from sturdy paper or cardboard. Transfer all markings.

2. Trace around the pattern pieces on the back of the fur.

You will need to draw:

On the black fur:

Piece 10 (Ear)—four

Piece 66 (Eye Patch)—one right and one left

Piece 67 (Upper Body Front)—one

Piece 69 (Lower Body Front)—one

Piece 70 (Upper Body Front)—one right and one left

Piece 72 (Lower Body Back)—one right and one left

On the white fur:

Piece 64 (Head Back)—one right and one left

Piece 65 (Head Front)—one right and one left

Piece 68 (Middle Body Front)—one

Piece 71 (Middle Body Back)—one right and one left

3. Cut out the fur pieces.

Remember: Do *not* cut the notches or the mouth lines.

4. Zig-zag stitch the mouths, starting at A.

5. Appliqué the *eye patches* on the head front.

Brush the fur away from the edges of the *eye patches*. Make a snip for the eye in both the patches and the head fronts. Stick crystal *eyes* through the holes in the *eye patches* and then through the holes in the head fronts (*do not* put the washer on the eye pegs yet). Make sure the fabric side of the patch is next to the fur side of the head front. Line up the *eye patches* as illustrated on the pattern. Pin both *eye patches* before you start to sew either one of them (see Figure 1). The exact placement of the *eye patches* is not important, but it is important that both *eye patches* are lined up. Remove the crystal *eye*. Zig-zag stitch around the eye patch, using a stitch width of about half the maximum width, and a stitch length a little longer than you use for zig-zagging the mouth (see Figure 2). You may need to stop frequently and use a pin to smooth the pile under the presser foot.

When you have the *eye patches* sewed on, the worst is over for the Panda,

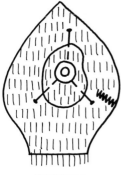

FIGURE 1

FIGURE 2

though I wouldn't say that sewing the body fronts and backs is *easy*.

6. Pin and sew the right and left head fronts together from B to C.

7. Sew on a ball fringe nose at D.

8. Pin and sew the ears.

9. Pin and sew the ears to each side of the head front between E and F.

10. Insert the eyes.

11. Pin and sew the head backs together from B to G.

12. Pin and sew the head back to the head front from H to B to H. Turn head right side out and set aside.

13. Assemble the body front.

On the table line up pieces 67, 68, and 69 (the upper, middle, and lower body fronts) matching letters and notches (see Figure 3). Check with the pattern if you have trouble figuring out what is going on. With the middle body front towards you, pin it to the upper body front, matching R's and notch V. Sew with the upper body front up and the

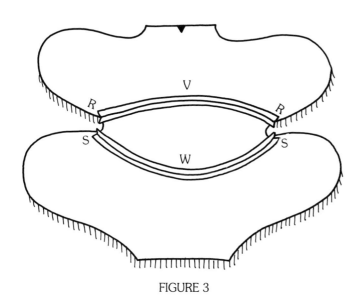

FIGURE 3

middle body front down. With the middle body front again facing towards you, pin it to the lower body front, matching S's and notch W. Sew with lower body front up and middle body front down.

14. Assemble the right and left body backs.

Use the same procedure for the backs that you did for the front, i.e., arrange the pieces on the table first so that the lefts are together and the rights are together, making sure they are all in the proper order. With the middle body back towards you when you pin, pin and sew it first to the upper body back, then to the lower body back (see Figure 4). Repeat for the other half of the back. (About this time you may be wondering why you wanted to make a Panda in the first place!)

15. Pin and sew the body backs to the body front from J to K to L.

16. Trim the seam allowance at J and K, as indicated by the dotted lines on the pattern.

17. Pin and sew the head to the body from M to C to M.

Remember: The head is right side out and tucked inside the body (which is still wrong side out), so that the pile sides of the fur are facing.

18. Turn the head wrong side out again.

19. Pin and sew the back seam from G to M to O.

20. Turn the puppet right side out.

21. Stuff the head.

22. Play with the puppet.

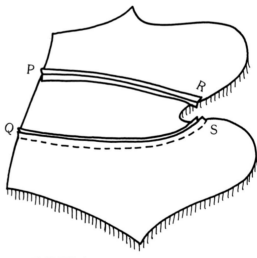

FIGURE 4

Skunk

All the skunk "experts" will tell you that the stripes on the tail should be more this way or whichever way. But the animal guidebook that I checked said there is a wide variation in the stripes of different skunks. Most people don't bother to check out a skunk's stripes when they meet one, anyway.

Materials

BODY: Short pile (³⁄₁₆″–¼″) to medium pile (⁵⁄₁₆″–³⁄₈″) fur in both black and white. Plush fur in a medium pile looks best, but it is often hard to find, especially the white.

TAIL: Fantasy fur (also called craft fur) in both black and white.

EARS: Black velour.

NOSE: Small black ball fringe (½″).

EYES: 15 mm brown crystal eyes.

STUFFING: About 1 oz. of polyester stuffing.

1. Trace and cut out the necessary pattern pieces.

For the Skunk you will need to trace pattern pieces 2, 6, 79, 80, 81, 82, 83, 84, 85, 86, and 87 from Section VII. Cut patterns from sturdy paper or cardboard. Transfer all markings.

2. Trace around the pattern pieces on the back of the fur.

You will need to draw:

On the short black fur:

Piece 2 (Body Front)—one

Piece 80 (Head Front)—one right and one left

Piece 85 (Body Back Gusset)—one

Piece 87 (Body Back)—one right and one left

On the short white fur:

Piece 79 (Head Back)—one right and one left

Piece 81 (Head Stripe)—one

Piece 86 (Body Back Stripe)—one right and one left

On the black fantasy fur:

Piece 82 (Tail Top)—one

Piece 83 (Tail Bottom)—one right and one left

On the white fantasy fur:

Piece 84 (Tail Stripe)—one right and one left

3. Cut out the fur pieces.

Remember: Do not cut out the notches or the mouth lines.

4. Cut out the velour pieces.

You will need to pin and cut out:

Piece 6 (Ear)—four (two pair)

5. Zig-zag stitch the mouth lines on the head fronts, starting at A.

Use gray thread (instead of the usual black), so that the mouth will show up on the black fur.

6. Pin and sew the head stripe to one head front.

Pin one edge of the head stripe to one head front between B and D, pile sides together. Sew ⅛″ from the edge (see Figure 1). Fold the head stripe in half and pin it to the same edge you just

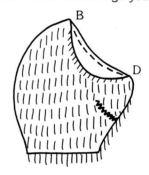

FIGURE 1

Ram

Rams are quite hard-headed, a characteristic of the males of many species. These rams have nothing to do all day but sit in a bed of clover and be charming.

Materials

BODY: Lambswool in any natural color. Warning: Never brush lambswool!

UPPER HEAD FRONT: Short pile (³⁄₁₆″–¼″) fur, or corduroy, in a color that coordinates with the lambswool.

HORNS, SOLES: Velour, in a color that looks good with the lambswool and face fur, or black, if no other color looks right.

NOSE: Small black ball fringe (½″).

EYES: 15 mm brown crystal eyes.

STUFFING: About 1 oz. of polyester stuffing.

1. Trace and cut out the necessary pattern pieces.

For the Ram you will need to trace pattern pieces 88, 89, 90, 91, 92, 93, 94, 95, 96, and 97 from Section VII. Cut patterns from sturdy paper or cardboard. Transfer all markings.

2. Trace around the pattern pieces on the back of the fur.

You will need to draw:

On the lambswool:

Piece 92 (Lower Head Front)—one right and one left

Piece 93 (Tail)—one right and one left

Piece 94 (Head Back)—one right and one left

Piece 96 (Body Front)—one

Piece 97 (Body Back)—one right and one left

On the short fur or corduroy:

Piece 95 (Upper Head Front)—one right and one left

3. Cut out the fur pieces.

Remember: *Do not cut the notches or the mouth lines.*

4. Cut out the velour pieces.

You will need to trace, cut out, and mark:

Piece 88 (Horn)—one right and one left (one pair)

Piece 89 (Horn)—one right and one left (one pair)

Piece 90 (Horn)—one right and one left (one pair)

Piece 91 (Sole)—four (two pairs). Mark the notches on these after you cut them out.

Remember that the velour has a nap, so make sure that the arrows on all the pattern pieces point in the same direction.

5. Zig-zag stitch the mouth lines on the upper head fronts, starting at A.

6. Match up the horns to the head pieces and pin and sew them in place.

There are three sections to each horn, and each section is attached to a separate piece of the head. I must admit, I can't remember where the horns go without checking the pattern pieces.

On a table lay out all the head pieces with their patterns, and all the horn pieces with their patterns. With the

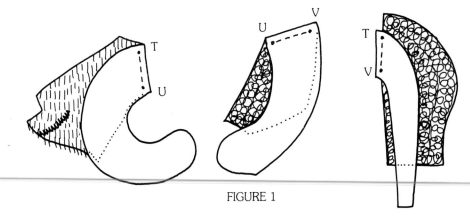

FIGURE 1

patterns on top of each piece, match letters to see which horn goes where. Make sure that when you put the right sides together you still have the letters right—it is easy to reverse things without realizing it.

When you get through matching everything, double-check, to make sure that each left head piece is a mirror image of the corresponding right head piece. Pin and sew the horns to the head pieces. (Remember: Do not brush lambswool.) Sew only from dot to dot (see Figure 1), as this will make it a little easier to do steps 9, 10, and 11.

7. Pin and sew the muzzle darts in the left and right upper head fronts from X to Y.

8. Pin and sew each head back to the corresponding lower head front from H to V to W.

Have the lower head front facing towards you when you pin. Stop at the dot at W when you sew (see Figure 2). Remember: *do not brush lambswool.*

9. Pin and sew the tops of the upper head fronts to the head backs from B to T to W.

Note: The seam from B to T is very short. Have the upper head front to-

wards you when you pin. Stop at the dot at W when you sew (see Figure 3).

10. Pin and sew the upper head fronts to the lower head fronts from Z to U to W.

Have the Z to your right when you pin. Sew, ending at the dot at W (see Figure 4).

11. Pin and sew the left head to the right head, from G to B to Z to C (see Figure 5).

12. Sew on a ball fringe nose at D.

13. Insert the eyes.

Turn head right side out and set aside.

14. Pin and sew the body backs to the body front from J to P, from Q to K to R, and from S to L.

Leave the ends of the legs open for inserting the soles (see Figure 6).

15. Trim the seam allowance at J and K, as indicated on the pattern.

16. Pin and sew the velour soles on the leg openings.

You may shudder at the thought of sewing soles on the bottoms of the legs, but don't despair. There is one method that is tedious, but not too aggravating (see Figure 7).

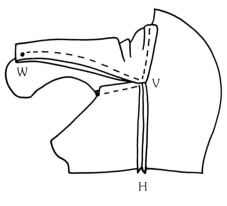

FIGURE 2

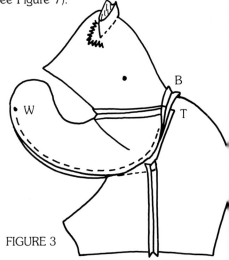

FIGURE 3

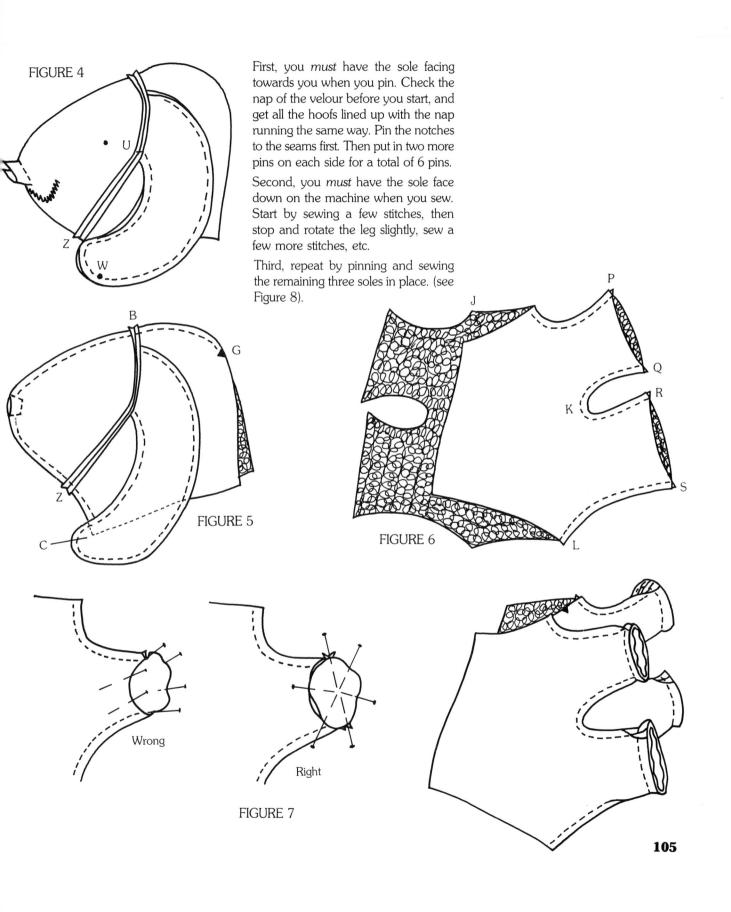

FIGURE 4

First, you *must* have the sole facing towards you when you pin. Check the nap of the velour before you start, and get all the hoofs lined up with the nap running the same way. Pin the notches to the seams first. Then put in two more pins on each side for a total of 6 pins.

Second, you *must* have the sole face down on the machine when you sew. Start by sewing a few stitches, then stop and rotate the leg slightly, sew a few more stitches, etc.

Third, repeat by pinning and sewing the remaining three soles in place. (see Figure 8).

FIGURE 5

FIGURE 6

Wrong

Right

FIGURE 7

105

17. Pin and sew the head to the body from H to C to H.

Remember: The head is right side out and tucked down inside the body, which is still wrong side out.

18. Turn the head wrong side out again.

19. Pin and sew the tail.

This tail does not have to be stuffed.

20. Pin and sew the tail to one body back.

21. Pin and sew the back seam from G to M to O.

22. Turn the puppet right side out.

Push the horns through into the head, then the head through into the body, and continue as usual.

23. Stuff the head.

You will have to stuff the horns first. Use *very* small pieces of stuffing, and pack them in firmly. A ball-point pen with the cap on works well for stuffing the horns. After the horns are stuffed, stuff the rest of the head.

24. Play with the puppet.

Turtle

These turtles are the only five-finger puppets that will sit up by themselves (because of their stuffed shells). For the shells you can experiment with corduroy fabric. Try wide-wale, narrow-wale, or no-wale fabric. I've even made turtles with striped or floral corduroy shells.

Materials

BODY: Medium pile ($5/16''$–$3/8''$) fur in any turtle color—brown, beige, rust, green.

SHELL, SOLES: Corduroy to complement the fur. It can be a solid color or a print.

EYES: 15 mm brown crystal eyes.

STUFFING: About 1 oz. of polyester stuffing.

1. Trace and cut out the necessary pattern pieces.

For the Turtle you will need to trace pieces 3, 4, 91, 96, 97, 98, 99, 100, 101 from Section VII. Cut patterns from sturdy paper or cardboard. Transfer all markings.

2. Trace around the pattern pieces on the back of the fur.

You will need to draw:

Piece 3 (Head Front)—one right and one left. (You will need to mark the mouth lines, but you can ignore the notches at D, E, and F, as the Turtle has no ears or nose.)

Piece 4 (Head Back)—one right and one left

Piece 96 (Body Front)—one

Piece 97 (Body Back)—one right and one left

3. Cut out the fur pieces.

4. Cut out the corduroy pieces.

You will need to pin, cut out, and mark:

Piece 91 (Sole)—four (two pairs)

Piece 98 (Back Shell Center)—one right and one left (one pair)

Piece 99 (Back Shell Sides)—two right and two left (two pairs)

Piece 100 (Back Shell Lining)—one right and one left (one pair)

Piece 101 (Shell Front)—two (one pair)

Remember: Corduroy has a nap, so make sure that the arrows on all pattern pieces are aligned with the grain of the fabric. After you have cut out the corduroy pieces, use a pen to mark the notches.

5. Zig-zag stitch the mouth lines on the head fronts, starting at A.

6. Pin and sew the head fronts together from B to C.

7. Pin and sew the head backs together from G to B.

8. Pin and sew the head back to the head front from H to B to H. Turn head right side out and set aside.

9. Pin and sew the body backs to the body front from J to P, from Q to K to R, and from S to L. Trim seam allowance at J and K as indicated on pattern.

10. Pin and sew the soles on the ends of the legs (see Figures 1 and 2).

Check the nap on the soles and line them up the same way as the shell. Have the soles towards you when you pin. Match the notches on the soles with the seams on the legs first, then add two more pins on each side. Have the soles face down on the machine when you sew. Every few stitches, stop

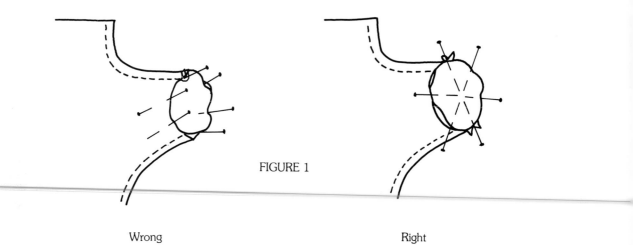

FIGURE 1

Wrong   Right

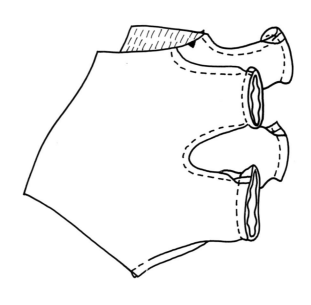

FIGURE 2

108

sewing and rotate the leg, so that it is out of the way of the stitching.

11. Pin and sew the head to the body from M to C to M.

Remember: The head is right side out and tucked down inside the body, which is still wrong side out.

12. Turn the head wrong side out again.

13. Pin and sew the back seam from G to M to O.

14. Turn the puppet right side out.

15. Pin and sew the shell fronts together.

Pin and sew the shell fronts together from T to U to T, from V to W, from X to Z, from Y to X, and from W to V (see Figure 3). Put double pins in at both Y and Z, and they will remind you that you have to stop sewing there and leave an opening for turning.

Trim the seam allowances on the shell front, as indicated on the pattern, but *do not* trim seam allowance at opening between Y and Z.

Turn the shell front right side out, through the opening between Y and Z.

Top-stitch the shell front (see Figure 4). Make sure that the seam allowance is tucked in evenly and pinned at the opening Y to Z. Topstitch ⅛″ from the edge, from X to X, from W to V, from T to U to T, and from V to W. (You need not sew the opening Y to Z shut by hand, as the topstitching will close it.)

16. Pin and sew the back shell linings together from BB to BB.

17. Pin and sew the shell front to the back shell lining.

With the shell front on the right side of the shell lining, pin, putting tabs X-W between notches X and W, and tabs V-T between notches V and T. Stitch ⅛″ from the end of each tab.

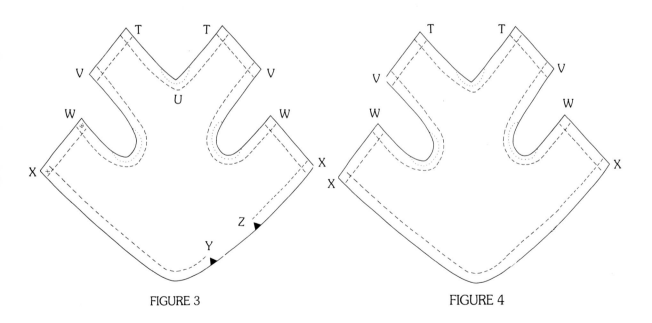

FIGURE 3   FIGURE 4

Note: The shell front will not lie completely flat on the back shell lining.

18. Assemble the back shell.

Using a pair of side shells, pin one side shell to one center shell, from DD to CC (right sides together). Sew, ending at the dot at DD (see Figure 5). Pin the other side shell to the center shell (right sides together), again matching DD and CC. Sew, ending at the dot at DD (see Figure 6). Repeat with the other center shell and pair of side shells.

Pin the two shell halves together from BB to DD to BB, and sew as one continuous seam (see Figure 7).

19. Pin and sew the back shell to the back shell lining.

With the back shell wrong side out, place it over the back shell lining (the shell front will be on the inside). Have the back shell lining towards you when you pin and face down when you sew. Match the seams at BB at each end first, and the notches X and W, then

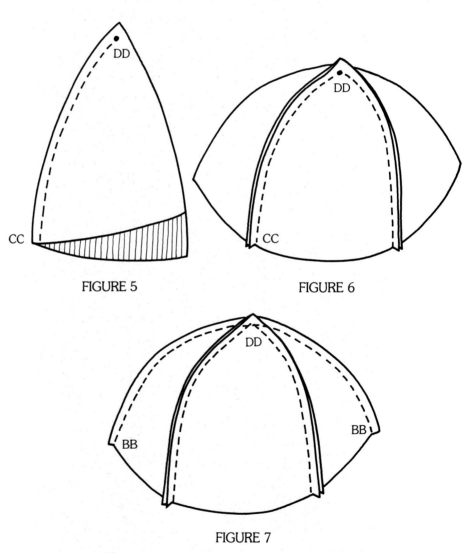

FIGURE 5

FIGURE 6

FIGURE 7

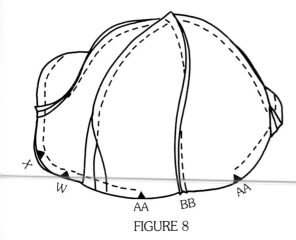

FIGURE 8

pin the rest of the way around the edges. *Note:* If you have X and W backwards, the edges won't match right.

Put in all the pins to start with, so that you can get the sides properly lined up, then remove the pins between the two AA's to leave an opening for turning. If you use double pins at the AA's, it will remind you to stop sewing there. Start at one AA and sew all the way around the shell to the other AA (see Figure 8).

20. Turn the shell right side out.

Start at the edge the farthest away from the opening, and push it through the opening.

21. Slip the shell on the turtle.

Put the head through the hole at T-U-T, and the front legs through the holes from V to W.

22. Stuff the head.

23. Tack down the shell at the mark X.

24. Stuff the shell.

Stuff the shell very lightly. It should be puffy, rather than firm. It is actually much harder to stuff something soft, than it is to stuff something firm. Push the stuffing all the way out to the edges of the shell—but push it gently! Don't ram it in. Also, try on the puppet frequently, to make sure that you are not getting so much stuffing in the shell that it interferes with putting your hand in the puppet. While your hand is still in the puppet, shape the shell so that it curves around your hand.

25. Sew the shell shut.

Use button-and-carpet thread, doubled and knotted, to sew the shell shut. The best stitch for sewing a stuffed animal shut is the ladder stitch, also called the slipstitch. Starting at the right end of the opening if you are right-handed, and at the left end if you are left-handed, fold over the seam allowance and run the needle through the folded edge, from the inside out, so that the knot will be inside the shell (see Figure 9).

Then (always keeping the needle pointed to the left) take a stitch about ¼″ long on the other side of the opening from where the knot is. Make the stitch along what would be the seam line, i.e., ¼″ from the edge of the fabric. Then take a stitch on the first side again, at the seam line, then back to the second side (see Figure 10).

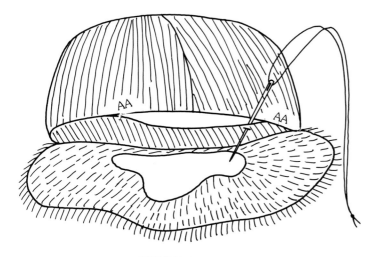

FIGURE 9

FIGURE 10

112

The threads going back and forth across the opening should go straight across, not at an angle (you can see why this is called the ladder stitch).

After two or three stitches, pull on the thread until the edges of the opening are shut. Don't pull so hard that you pucker the seam. Continue taking two or three stitches, then pulling the thread tight.

When you get to the end of the opening, knot the thread by making a loop and running the needle through the loop and pulling it tight. Three times through three loops makes a good knot that won't come undone. Do not cut the thread yet. Instead, insert the needle right next to the knot and poke it out about an inch from the knot. Pulling on the thread gently, clip the thread where it comes out of the shell. This keeps the ends of the thread from being visible, while at the same time keeping the ends long enough that the knot won't come undone.

26. Play with the puppet.

Besides the usual things that you can do with a five-finger puppet, you can also make the Turtle get stuck on his back, or rock on his shell, trying to turn over (but don't leave him stuck on his back too long!)

Stuffed Animals

Making a stuffed animal is a little harder than making the equivalent puppet, in several ways. The darts in the body front make sewing the body front to the body backs a bit more difficult, the opening for turning the animal right side out is much smaller, the whole animal has to be stuffed rather than just the head, and the animal must then be sewed shut. On the other hand, making a simple stuffed animal such as the Prairie Dog is still much easier than making a complicated puppet, such as the Skunk, and if you have little people around, the stuffed animals are more huggy than the puppets.

Before you start making a stuffed animal, please make the Prairie Dog puppet at the beginning of the book, even if you don't want a puppet. It doesn't take much fur or much time, and it will teach you what you need to know about working with fake fur. Assuming you have already done that, you are ready to make a stuffed animal.

Materials

Refer to the materials list for each animal as given in sections I, II, III, IV, and V.

Note: If making the Squirrel, Fox, or Skunk for a small child, it is better not to choose the fantasy fur (craft fur) option for the animal's tail, as this material does not hold up well under heavy handling or chewing and it also does not wash well, if the need arises. If no other shag is available, use the same short fur for the tail that you use for the body.

1. Trace and cut out the necessary pattern pieces.

Note: The darts in pieces 102, 103, 110, 111, and 117 are cut out of the paper pattern *only*. Use the pattern as a stencil for marking the stitching lines on the back of the fur, the same way you mark the mouth lines, notches, and eye positions. *Do not* cut the darts out of the fur.

For the **Prairie Dog** you will need to trace and cut out pattern pieces 3, 4, 5, 6, 102, & 103 from Section VII.
For the **Squirrel**—pieces 3, 4, 6, 7, 102, 103.
For the **Bear**—pieces 8, 9, 10, 102, 103.
For the **Lion**—10, 11, 12, 13, 14, 102, 103.
For the **Rabbit**—9, 15, 16, 102, 103.
For the **Mouse**—9, 17, 18, 102, 103.
For the **Dog**—9, 19, 20, 21, 102, 103.
For the **Cat**—22, 23, 24, 25, 102, 103.

For the **Possum**—27, 28, 29, 102, 103.
For the **Hedgehog**—27, 28, 29, 102, 103.
For the **Koala**—29, 30, 31, 32, 102, 103.
For the **Monkey**—27, 33, 34, 35, 36, 102, 103.
For the **Raccoon**—37, 38, 39, 40, 41, 42, 43, 44, 45, 46, 102, 103.
For the **Fox**—47, 48, 49, 52, 53, 54, 55, 103, 104, 105.
For the **Dragon**—56, 57, 58, 59, 60, 61, 103, 104, 105.
For the **Alligator**—58, 59, 60, 61, 103, 104, 105.
For the **Panda**—10, 64, 65, 66, 106, 107, 108, 109, 110, 111.
For the **Ladybug**—74, 76, 77, 78, 102, 112, 113.
For the **Skunk**—6, 79, 80, 81, 82, 83, 84, 102, 114, 115, 116.
For the **Ram**—88, 89, 90, 91, 92, 93, 94, 95, 117, 118.
For the **Turtle**—3, 4, 91, 98, 99, 100, 101, 117, 118.

2. Trace around the pattern pieces on the back of the fur.

For the **Prairie Dog** you will need to draw:

Piece 3 (Head Front)—one right and one left

Piece 4 (Head Back)—one right and one left

Piece 5 (Tail)—one right and one left

Piece 102 (Body Front)—one

Piece 103 (Body Back)—one right and one left

For the **Squirrel** you will need to draw:

On the short fur:

Piece 3 (Head Front)—one right and one left

Piece 4 (Head Back)—one right and one left

Piece 102 (Body Front)—one

Piece 103 (Body Back)—one right and one left

On the shag fur:

Piece 7 (Tail)—one right and one left

For the **Bear** you will need to draw:

Piece 8 (Head Front)—one right and one left

Piece 9 (Head Back)—one right and one left

Piece 10 (Ear)—four

Piece 102 (Body Front)—one

Piece 103 (Body Back)—one right and one left

For the **Lion** you will need to draw:

On the short fur:

Piece 10 (Ear)—four

Piece 11 (Head Front)—one right and one left

Piece 13 (Tail)—one

Piece 102 (Body Front)—one

Piece 103 (Body Back)—one right and one left

On the shag fur:

Piece 12 (Head Back)—one right and one left

Piece 14 (Tip of Tail)—one

For the **Rabbit** you will need to draw:

Piece 9 (Head Back)—one right and one left

Piece 15 (Head Front)—one right and one left

Piece 16 (Ear)—two

Piece 102 (Body Front)—one

Piece 103 (Body Back)—one right and one left

For the **Mouse** you will need to draw:

Piece 9 (Head Back)—one right and one left

Piece 17 (Head Front)—one right and one left

Piece 102 (Body Front)—one

Piece 103 (Body Back)—one right and one left

For the **Dog** you will need to draw:

Piece 9 (Head Back)—one right and one left

Piece 19 (Head Front)—one right and one left

Piece 20 (Tail)—one

Piece 21 (Ear)—one right and one left

Piece 102 (Body Front)—one

Piece 103 (Body Back)—one right and one left

For the **Cat** you will need to draw:

Piece 22 (Head Front)—one right and one left

Piece 23 (Ear)—two rights and two lefts

Piece 24 (Tail)—one

Piece 25 (Head Back)—one right and one left

Piece 102 (Body Front)—one

Piece 103 (Body Back)—one right and one left

For the **Possum** you will need to draw:

Piece 27 (Head Back)—one right and one left

Piece 103 (Body Back)—one right and one left

For the **Hedgehog** you will need to draw: (remember that the pile strokes *up* on the Hedgehog)

Piece 27 (Head Back)—one right and

one left

Piece 103 (Body Back)—one right and one left

For the **Koala** you will need to draw:

On the body fur:

Piece 29 (Ear)—two

Piece 30 (Head Back)—one right and one left

Piece 31 (Ear)—two

Piece 32 (Head Front)—one right and one left

Piece 102 (Body Front)—one

Piece 103 (Body Back)—one right and one left

On the white fur:

Piece 31 (Ear)—two

For the **Monkey** you will need to draw:

Piece 27 (Head Back)—one right and one left

Piece 34 (Lower Face)—one right and one left

Piece 36 (Tail)—one

Piece 102 (Body Front)—one

Piece 103 (Body Back)—one right and one left

For the **Raccoon** you will need to draw:

On the brown fur:

Piece 37 (Ear)—two

Piece 40 (Second Tail Stripe)—one

Piece 42 (Fourth Tail Stripe)—one

Piece 44 (Head Back)—one right and one left

Piece 46 (Upper Head Front)—one right and one left

Piece 102 (Body Front)—one

Piece 103 (Body Back)—one right and one left

On the black fur:

Piece 38 (Eye Patch)—one right and one left

Piece 39 (First Tail Stripe)—one

Piece 41 (Third Tail Stripe)—one

Piece 43 (Fifth Tail Stripe)—one

On the white fur:

Piece 45 (Lower Head Front)—one right and one left

For the **Fox** you will need to draw:

On the rust fur:

Piece 49 (Upper Head Front)—one right and one left

Piece 52 (Ear)—one right and one left

Piece 54 (Tail)—two (option—cut this of rust fantasy fur)

Piece 55 (Head Back)—one right and one left

Piece 103 (Body Back)—one right and one left

Piece 105 (Front Legs)—one right and one left

On the white fur:

Piece 47 (Tail Tip)—two (option—cut this of white fantasy fur)

Piece 48 (Lower Head Front)—one right and one left

Piece 104 (Chest)—one

For the **Dragon** or the **Alligator** you will need to draw:

On the main color fur:

Piece 58 (Head Back)—one right and one left

Piece 59 (Tail)—one right and one left

Piece 61 (Upper Head Front)—one (mark the dart P-P, but don't cut it out)

Piece 103 (Body Back)—one right and one left

Piece 105 (Front Legs)—one right and one left

On the contrasting color fur:

Piece 60 (Lower Head Front)—one

Piece 104 (Chest)—one

For the **Panda** you will need to draw:

On the black fur:

Piece 10 (Ear)—four

Piece 66 (Eye Patch)—one right and one left

Piece 108 (Lower Body Back)—one right and one left

Piece 109 (Upper Body Back)—one right and one left

Piece 110 (Upper Body Front)—one

Piece 111 (Lower Body Front)—one

On the white fur:

Piece 64 (Head Back)—one right and one left

Piece 65 (Head Front)—one right and one left

Piece 106 (Middle Body Front)—one

Piece 107 (Middle Body Back)—one right and one left

For the **Ladybug** you will need to draw:

On the gray fur:

Piece 77 (Head Front)—one right and one left

Piece 102 (Body Front)—one

Piece 113 (Leg Back)—one right and one left

On the reddish fur:

Piece 112 (Body Back)—one right and one left

On the black fur:

Piece 74 (Spot)—six

Piece 76 (Head Back)—one right and one left

For the **Skunk** you will need to draw:

On the short black fur:

Piece 80 (Head Front)—one right and one left

Piece 102 (Body Front)—one

Piece 114 (Body Back)—one right and one left

Piece 115 (Body Back Gusset)—one

On the short white fur:

Piece 79 (Head Back)—one right and one left

Piece 81 (Head Stripe)—one

Piece 116 (Body Back Stripe)—one right and one left

On the black fantasy fur:

Piece 82 (Tail Top)—one
Piece 83 (Tail Bottom)—one right and one left

On the white fantasy fur:

Piece 84 (Tail Stripe)—one right and one left

For the **Ram** you will need to draw:

Piece 92 (Lower Head Front)—one right and one left

Piece 93 (Tail)—one right and one left

Piece 94 (Head Back)—one right and one left

Piece 117 (Body Front)—one

Piece 118 (Body Back)—one right and one left

On the short fur or corduroy:

Piece 95 (Upper Head Front)—one right and one left

For the **Turtle** you will need to draw:

Piece 3 (Head Front)—one right and one left

Piece 4 (Head Back)—one right and one left

Piece 117 (Body Front)—one

Piece 118 (Body Back)—one right and one left

3. Cut out the fur pieces.

Remember: Do not cut out the notches, the darts, or the mouth lines. Mark them on the fur with a pen, but do not cut them out!

4. Trace and cut out the velour and corduroy pieces.

Remember: Both velour and corduroy have nap, so you will need to have all the arrows on the pattern pieces running the same way.

For the **Prairie Dog** you will need to pin and cut out:

Piece 6 (Ear)—four (two pairs)

For the **Squirrel** you will need to pin and cut out:

Piece 6 (Ear)—four (two pairs)

For the **Rabbit** you will need to pin and cut out:

Piece 16 (Ear)—two (one pair)

For the **Mouse** you will need to pin and cut out:

Piece 18 (Ear)—four (two pairs)

For the **Dog** you will need to pin and cut out:

Piece 21 (Ear)—one right and one left (one pair)

For the **Possum** you will need to pin and cut out:

From the dark velour:

Piece 29 (Ear)—four (two pairs)

From the light velour:

Piece 28 (Head Front)—one right and one left

Piece 102 (Body Front)—one

Note: Mark the notches, mouth lines, and eye positions on the velour with a pen after you have cut out the pieces.

For the **Hedgehog** you will need to pin and cut out:

From the velour:

Piece 29 (Ear)—four (two pairs)

From the corduroy:

Piece 28 (Head Front)—one right and one left

Piece 102 (Body Front)—one

Note: Mark the notches, mouth lines, and eye positions on the corduroy with a pen after you have cut out the pieces.

For the **Monkey** you will need to pin and cut out:

Piece 33 (Face)—one right and one left

Piece 35 (Ear)—two rights and two lefts (two pairs)

Note: Mark the notches, mouth lines, and eye positions on the velour with a pen after you have cut out the pieces.

For the **Raccoon** you will need to pin and cut out:

Piece 37 (Ear)—two (one pair)

For the **Fox** you will need to pin and cut out:

Piece 53 (Ear Lining)—one right and one left (one pair)

For the **Dragon** you will need to pin and cut out:

Piece 56 (Tail Bumps)—one left and one right

Piece 57 (Head Bumps)—one left and one right

Note: Mark the notches on the velour with a pen after you have cut the pieces out.

For the **Ladybug** you will need to pin and cut out:

Piece 78 (Antennae)—one

For the **Skunk** you will need to pin and cut out:

Piece 6 (Ear)—four (two pair)

For the **Ram** you will need to pin and cut out:

Piece 88 (Horn)—one right and one left

Piece 89 (Horn)—one right and one left

Piece 90 (Horn)—one right and one left

Piece 91 (Sole)—four (two pairs)—mark the notches on these after you cut them.

For the **Turtle** you will need to pin and cut out:

From corduroy:

Piece 91 (Sole)—four (two pairs)

Piece 98 (Back Shell - Center) — one right and one left

Piece 99 (Back Shell-Sides)—two rights and two lefts

Piece 100 (Back Shell-Lining)—one right and one left

Piece 101 (Shell Front)—two

Note: Mark all the notches on the corduroy with a pen after you have cut the pieces out.

5. Make the heads and tails according to the directions in Sections I, II, III, IV, and V. (For the Turtle, also make the shell). Remember to leave the back heads open from G to M. For the Skunk, also leave the tail open from V to O.

Note: In the following instructions for making the stuffed animal bodies, diagrams are given only for the Prairie Dog. To put together the body fronts and backs for the Fox, Dragon, Alligator, Panda, Ladybug, Skunk, Ram, and Turtle you may find it helpful to refer to the figures in the appropriate puppet section. Even though the shapes of the patterns are slightly different for the stuffed animals, the pieces are similar enough to the ones for the puppet bodies that you shouldn't have any trouble following the instructions.

6. For the **Prairie Dog, Squirrel, Bear, Lion, Rabbit, Mouse, Dog, Cat, Possum, Hedgehog, Koala, Monkey, Raccoon, Ladybug, Skunk, Ram,** and **Turtle,** stitch the four darts in the body front.

Fold the dart in half (see Figure 1), and pin. Sew the dart, using the pen lines as a stitching guide. Repeat for the other 3 darts.

6a. For the **Fox** and **Dragon,** pin and sew one front leg piece to the chest, from P to R, ending at the dot at R. Have the chest towards you when you pin and down when you sew. Then sew the other front leg piece to the chest from P to R, again ending at dot. Finally, sew the front legs together from the dot at R to S.

6b. For the **Alligator,** mark the lines across the chest with a pen, as indicated on the pattern, approximately an inch apart. Sew zig-zag black lines across the chest, as described in Step 11 under instructions for the Alligator puppet. Then proceed to sew the front legs to the chest, as described in Step 6a above.

6c. For the **Panda,** sew the upper body front to the middle body front. Then sew the lower body front to the middle body front. Each time, match the notches and have the middle body front facing towards you when you pin and down when you sew. After all three pieces are joined together properly, then sew the darts in the pieced body front as in Step 6 above.

7. For the **Prairie Dog, Squirrel, Bear, Lion, Rabbit, Mouse, Dog, Cat, Possum, Hedgehog, Koala, Monkey, Raccoon, Fox, Dragon, Alligator, Ram** and **Turtle,** sew the body backs together from CC to L (see Figure 2). This is one of those situations where you have to sew the body backs together *before* you can sew them to the body front, and you have to sew the body backs to the body front *before* you can sew the head onto the body. Then you have to have the body back seam open in order to sew the head to the body, but you've already sewed it shut! The only solution is to sew just enough of the body back seam together so that the body back can be sewed to the body front, while still leaving as much as possible of the seam open, so that the head and tail can be inserted later.

7a. For the **Panda,** first construct the body backs by sewing the upper body backs to the middle body backs, then sew the lower body backs to the middle body backs. Lay the pieces out in order on the table first, to make sure you don't mix them up. Have the middle body backs facing towards you when you pin and down when you sew. When left and right body backs are constructed, sew them together from CC to L as in Step 7 above.

7b. For the **Ladybug,** appliqué the spots on the body back as described in Step 13 under the instructions for making the Ladybug puppet. Then sew the leg back pieces to the body back from P to Q to R. Have the body back towards you when you pin and down when you sew. When both body backs are completed, sew them together from CC to L as in Step 7 above.

7c. For the **Skunk,** sew the body back stripes to the body backs from P to Q to R. Match the notches and have the stripes towards you when you pin and down when you sew. Sew the body back gusset to one body back stripe from dot at M to DD to S. Have the body back gusset towards you when you pin and down when you sew. Fi-

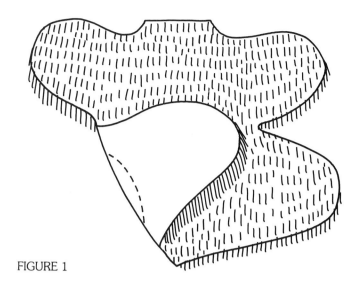

FIGURE 1

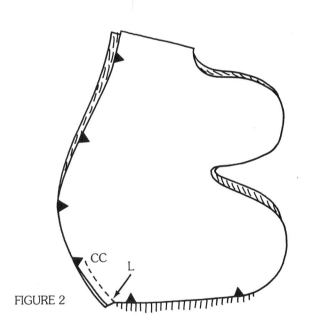

FIGURE 2

CC
L

nally, sew the body backs together from CC to L, as in Step 7 above.

8. For the **Prairie Dog, Bear, Lion, Rabbit, Mouse, Dog, Cat, Possum, Hedgehog, Koala, Monkey, Raccoon, Fox, Panda,** and **Ladybug,** sew the body back to the body front from J to K to FF to EE to L to EE to FF to K to J (see Figure 3). Because of the darts in the body front, it will be easier to stitch this seam if you have the body back towards you when you pin and down when you sew.

Be especially careful to take the correct seam allowance near the neck (as described in Step 15 under directions for making the Prairie Dog), or you will have trouble attaching the head to the body. The only other place you have to be careful is the body back seam at L. Make sure the seam allowance is open and flattened properly, so that it doesn't get pushed to one side as you sew.

8a. For the **Squirrel, Dragon, Alligator,** and **Skunk,** sew the body back to the body front from J to K to FF, leave an opening from FF to EE, then sew from EE to L to EE to FF to K to J. *Note:* It makes absolutely no difference whether the opening is on the right side or the left side. If you think you may forget to stop sewing and end up with no opening and have to rip out part of the seam, just put double pins at FF and EE, so that when you sew up to the double pins, you will remember to stop sewing and leave an opening.

The normal place to leave an opening for turning and stuffing is in the middle of the back. However for these animals, the tail takes up too much of the back seam, so the opening is left in the bottom of the leg. (Whenever you make a stuffed animal, the opening should be in the least conspicuous straight seam, as it is hard to hand sew a curved seam and make it look right.)

8b. For the **Ram,** sew the body front to the body back from J to P, from Q to K to R, from S to FF to EE to L to

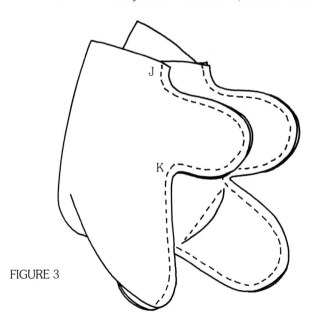

FIGURE 3

EE to FF to S, again from R to K to Q, and from P to J. Leave the ends of the legs open from P to Q and from R to S. Sew the soles on the ends of the legs according to the directions in Step 16 under directions for making the Ram puppet.

8c. For the **Turtle,** sew the body front to the body back from J to P, from Q to K to R, from S to FF. Leave an opening from FF to EE. Sew from EE to L to EE to FF to S. Because of the shell, the opening for turning and stuffing has to be in the bottom of the leg, as in Step 8a above. Then sew the soles onto the ends of the legs according to the directions in Step 10 under directions for making the Turtle puppet.

9. For **all animals,** trim the seam allowance at J and K, as indicated by the dotted lines on the pattern.

10. For **all animals,** sew the head to the body from M to J to C to J to M.

Note: The head should be right side out, and tucked down inside the body, so that the pile sides of the fur are together (see Figure 4). The body should be towards you when you pin, because you will be sewing the seam from inside the neck. After you are done sewing the head on the body, turn the head wrong side out again.

11. For the **Prairie Dog, Squirrel, Lion, Mouse, Dog, Cat, Possum, Monkey, Raccoon, Fox, Dragon, Alligator,** and **Ram,** sew the tail to one body back, with the bottom of the tail at notch N. Sew about ⅛″ from the edge of the fur, so that this seam will not accidentally show when you sew the regular ¼″ seam later. See directions for individual animals for more specific instructions and diagrams.

12. For the **Prairie Dog, Bear, Lion, Mouse, Dog, Cat, Possum, Hedgehog, Koala, Monkey, Raccoon, Fox, Panda, Ladybug,** and **Ram,** sew the center back seam from G to M to GG. Leave an opening for turning from GG to HH. Sew from HH to N to CC (see Figure 5). For the animals with tails, pin with the body back towards you which does *not* have the tail sewed to it. Then sew with the body back up that *does* have the tail sewed to it. This is so you can control the fur there, and keep it from rolling over and making an unwanted pleat.

12a. For the **Squirrel, Dragon, Alligator,** and **Turtle,** sew the center back

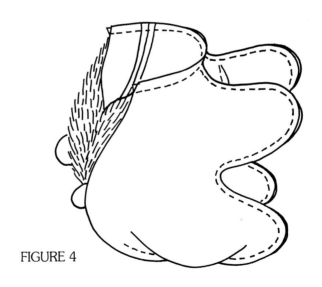

FIGURE 4

125

seam from G to M to GG to HH to N to CC. You do not need to leave an opening from GG to HH, as you have already left an opening for turning these animals in the bottom of one leg.

12b. For the **Rabbit,** sew the center back seam from HH to N to CC. Then sew the tail onto the body by hand, placing it so that the bottom edge of the tail will be positioned at N. Use the same method that you use for sewing on noses. Then sew the back seam together from G to M to GG.

12c. For the **Skunk,** sew the center back seam from G to M to DD to S. With the tail right side out, pin and sew to the body from O to R to S to S to R to O. (See Step 22 under directions for making the Skunk puppet.) Turn

the tail wrong-side out again, and sew the under-tail seam from V to O to CC.

13. For **all animals except the Turtle,** turn the animal right side out.

You will find that turning the stuffed animals right side out is more difficult than turning the puppets right side out, as the opening is much smaller. In general, the head is poked through the opening first, then each leg in turn. When the animal has a large tail, such as the **Skunk,** it is a toss-up as to whether you should push the tail or the head through first. (Whichever you pick, you'll decide you should have done the other first!) However, with a little careful struggling, persistence will pay off, and you can get the **Skunk** right side out.

13a. For the **Turtle,** turn it right side out as described above in Step 13, and then "put on" the shell, pushing the head through the neck opening and the front legs through the leg openings.

14. Stuff the animal.

Make sure you read the directions for stuffing in Step 23 under directions for making the Prairie Dog puppet. As a general rule, stuff the parts farthest from the opening first, i.e., the head first, (on the **Skunk** the tail comes second), next the legs, then the body. For animals with the opening in the lower leg, stuff the head first, then the upper legs and the chest, next the lower leg that doesn't have the opening, then the bottom, ending with the leg to be sewed shut.

Also, as a general rule, the head is stuffed more firmly than the body. To

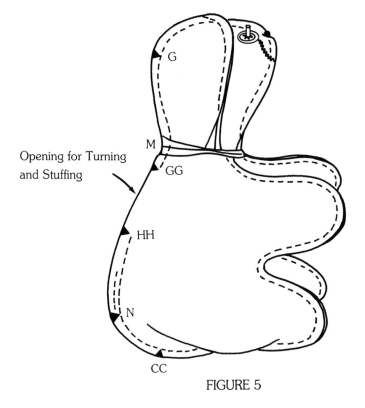

Opening for Turning and Stuffing

FIGURE 5

give you an idea of amounts, simple animals, like the Bear, will take about 2 oz. of stuffing or slightly less. Animals with large tails, horns, shells, etc., will take proportionately more. The **Turtle** shell can be stuffed lightly (about ¼ to ½ oz. of stuffing), as with the puppet, or more firmly (about 1 oz. of stuffing), whichever you prefer.

15. Sew the opening shut.

For complete directions on using the ladder stitch to sew an animal shut, see the directions for sewing the **Turtle** shell shut (Step 25). It will be harder to sew the stuffed animals shut than it is to sew a Turtle shell shut, because the fur gets in your way and makes it hard to see what you are doing.

You will also notice that when you stuff an animal, the pile near the opening gets shoved inside along with the stuffing. Before you start to sew the animal shut, you need to work all that pile back out. An old sewing machine needle works well for this job.

16. Washing the stuffed animal. (Optional)

If something should happen, and you need to wash the stuffed animal (we had a Penguin, that fell into the Gulf of Mexico three times), you do not need to unstuff it to wash it. If you have used the proper materials as directed in the instructions, and have not substituted something like felt for the velour, and have used polyester stuffing, then the whole animal should be washable. Most of the modern fake fur currently available to the home sewer is washable. The only furs I know of that are not, are fantasy fur (craft fur) and the super realistic fake mink, fake fox, fake ermine, etc., and other fake furs used by the coat industry. In any case, if a baby spits up or wets on an animal, it is either wash it or pitch it.

The best way to wash a stuffed animal is in a washing machine, because the spin cycle will extract most of the water and cut down on the chance of mildew. However, do not attempt to dry the animal in a dryer, unless you use air only. The heat from even a normal household dryer set on low temperature is still enough to frizzle the fake fur, so *air dry* only. Better yet, set the animal in the sun on a day when the humidity is low. If you spin dry the animal, it will usually finish air drying in less than 24 hours.

Do not expect to achieve an animal that looks brand-new. After a stuffed animal has been hugged and loved and played with, there is no technique that will restore it to its original pristine condition. Washing and brushing it will, however, improve it considerably.

VII. PATTERNS

Here are the patterns you'll need to make all of the puppets in the book. The last few patterns are the variations for stuffed animal bodies.

All of the patterns are actual-size so you can trace them right out of the book. If you're planning to make a lot of puppets, transfer the patterns onto cardboard or oaktag so that they will be sturdy and reusable.

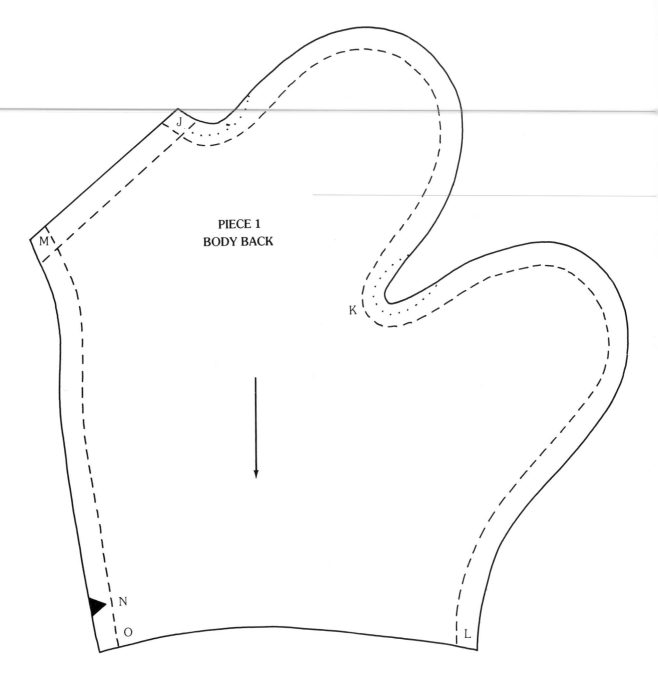

PIECE 1
BODY BACK

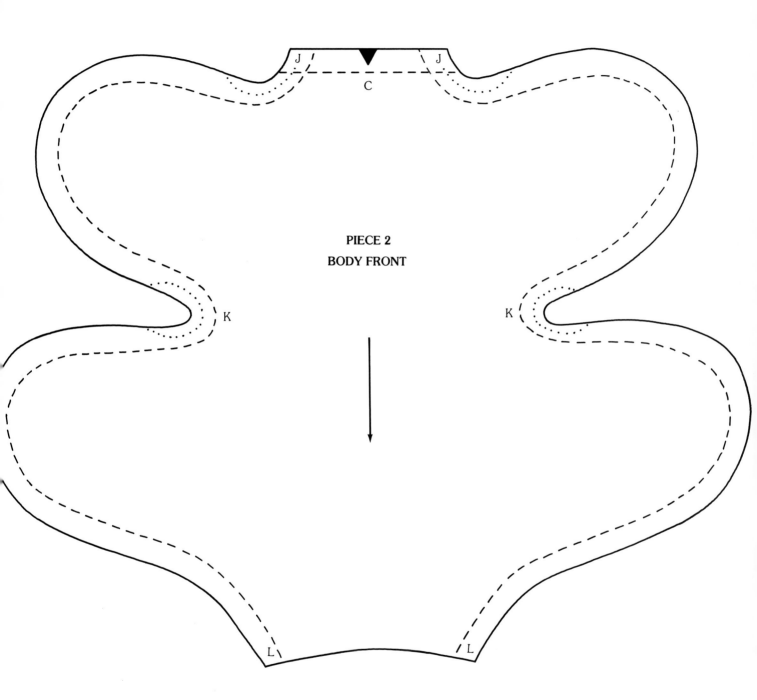

PIECE 2
BODY FRONT

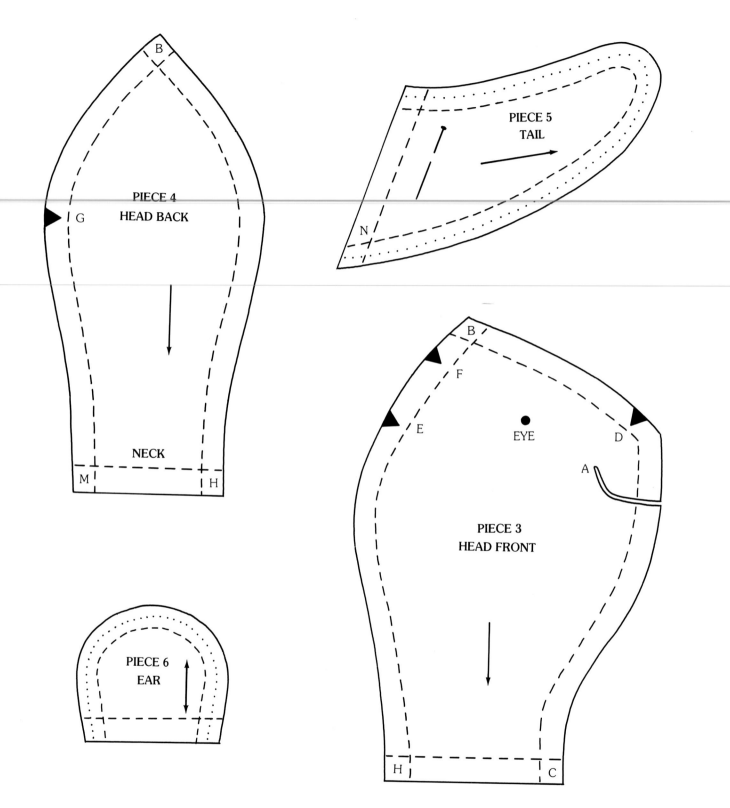

PIECE 4
HEAD BACK

PIECE 5
TAIL

PIECE 3
HEAD FRONT

EYE

NECK

PIECE 6
EAR

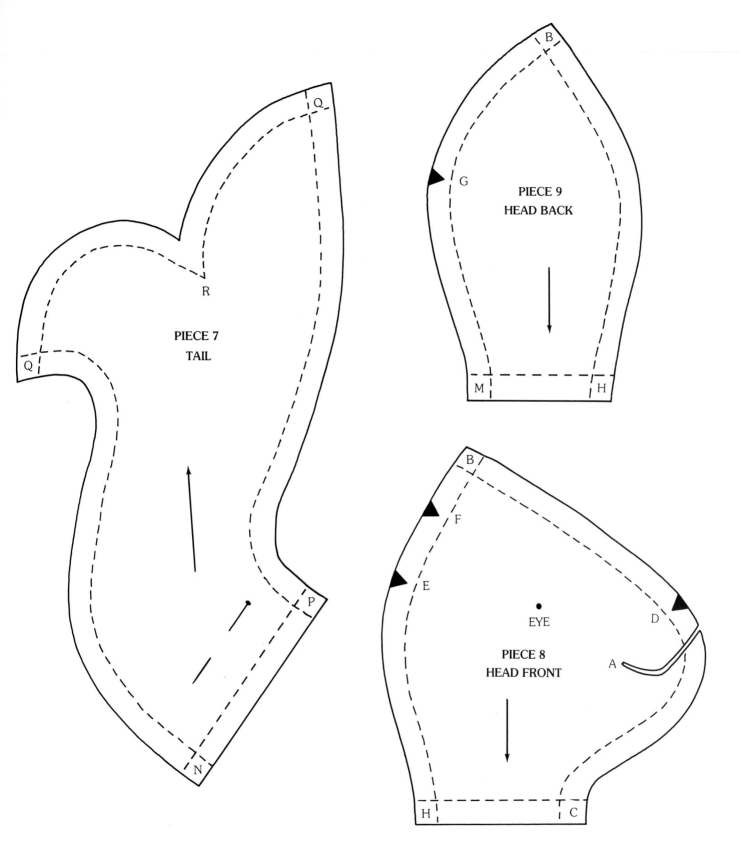

PIECE 7
TAIL

Q

R

Q

N

P

PIECE 9
HEAD BACK

B

G

M

H

PIECE 8
HEAD FRONT

B

F

E

EYE

D

A

H

C

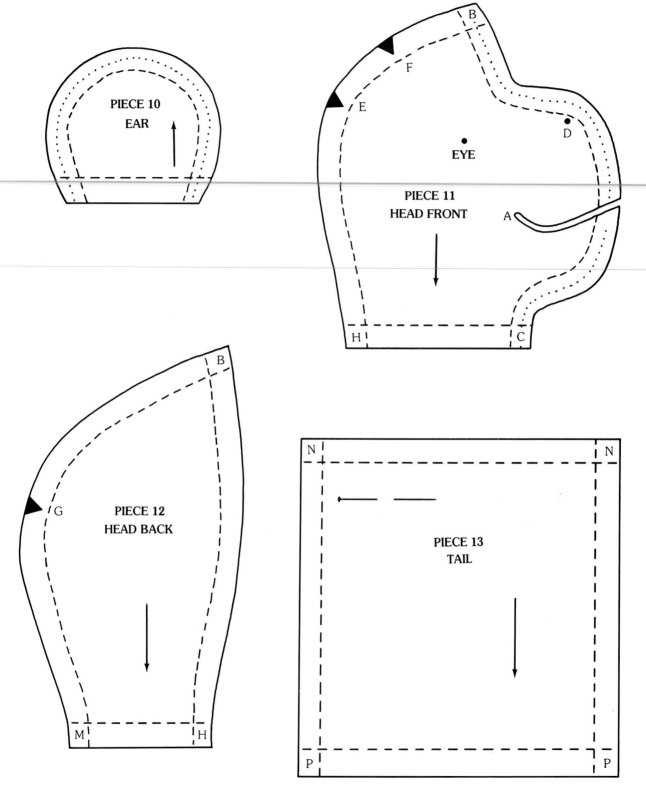

PIECE 10
EAR

PIECE 11
HEAD FRONT

EYE

A

B

F

E

D

H

C

PIECE 12
HEAD BACK

B

G

M

H

PIECE 13
TAIL

N

N

P

P

134

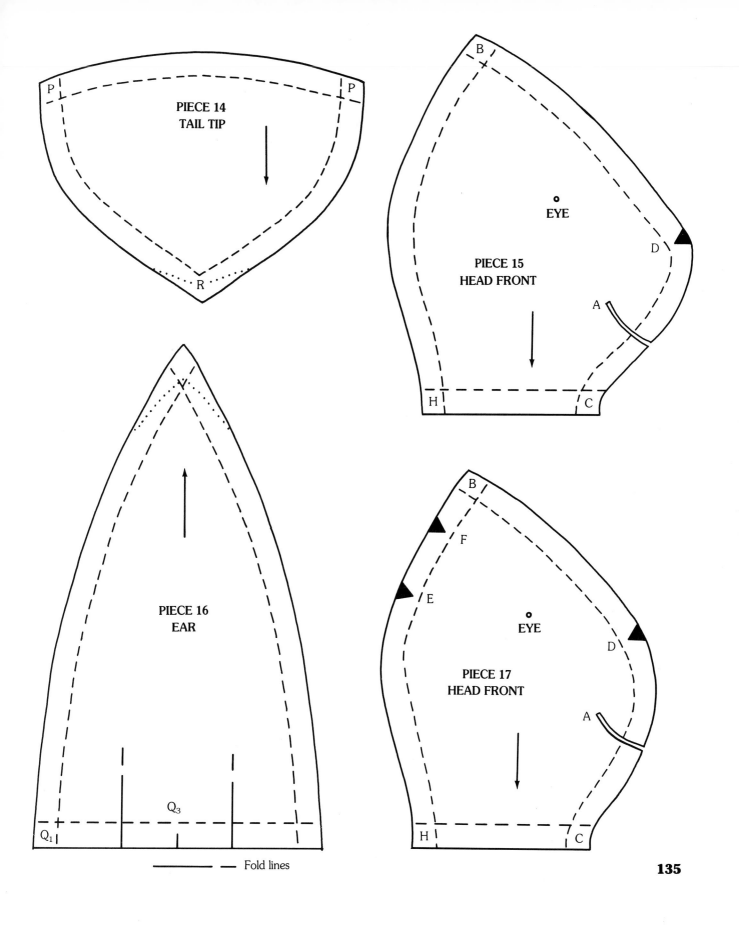

PIECE 14
TAIL TIP

P   P

R

PIECE 15
HEAD FRONT

EYE

B

D

A

H   C

PIECE 16
EAR

Q₃

Q₁

Fold lines

PIECE 17
HEAD FRONT

B

F

E

EYE

D

A

H   C

135

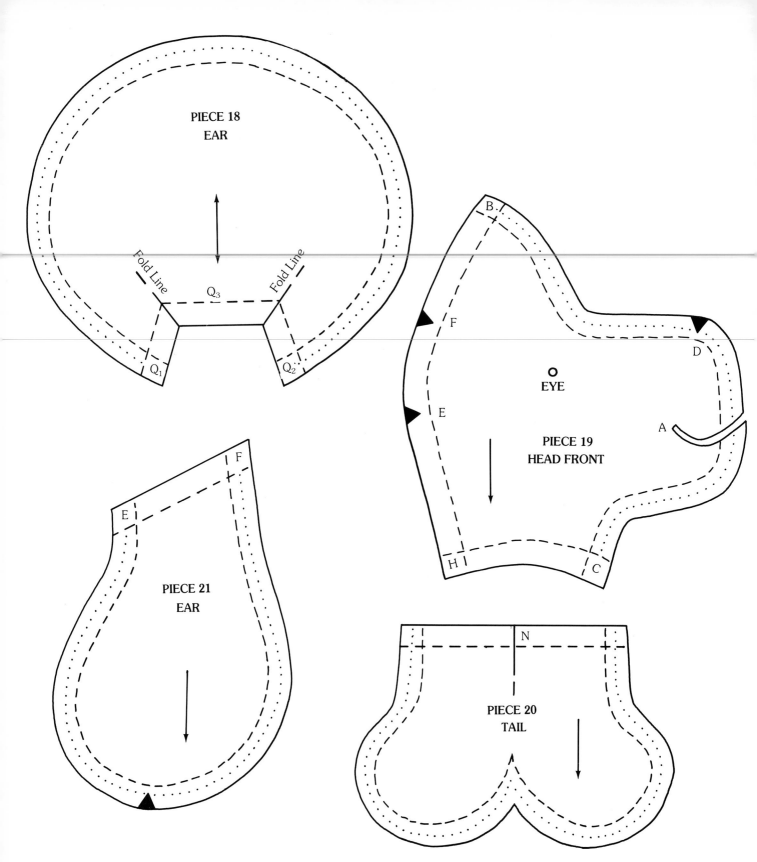

PIECE 18
EAR

Fold Line

Q_3

Fold Line

Q_1

Q_2

B

F

D

E

A

○
EYE

PIECE 19
HEAD FRONT

H

C

F

E

PIECE 21
EAR

N

PIECE 20
TAIL

136

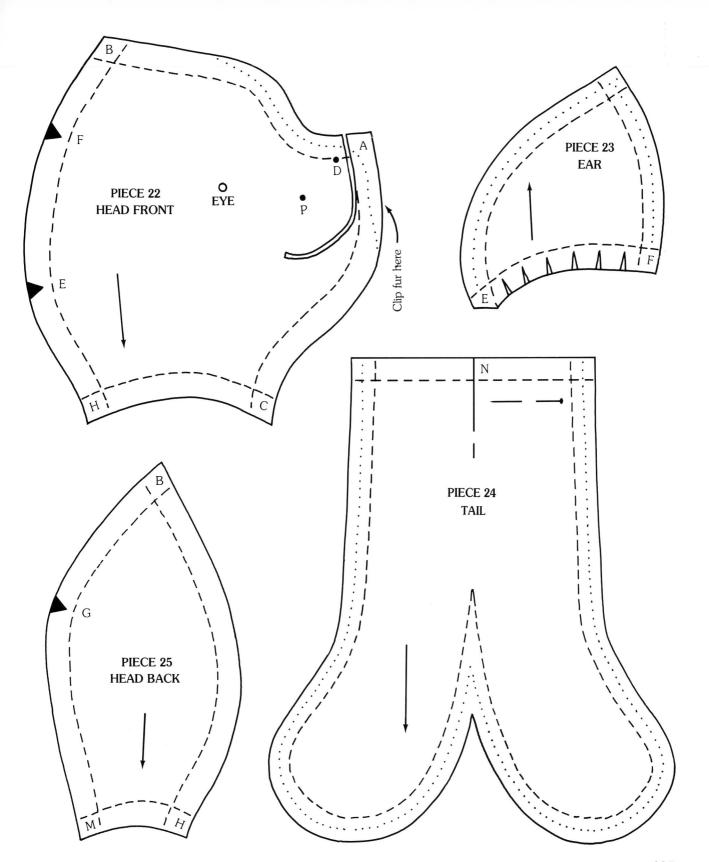

PIECE 22
HEAD FRONT

EYE

B

F

E

D

A

P

Clip fur here

H

C

PIECE 23
EAR

E

F

N

PIECE 24
TAIL

B

G

PIECE 25
HEAD BACK

M

H

137

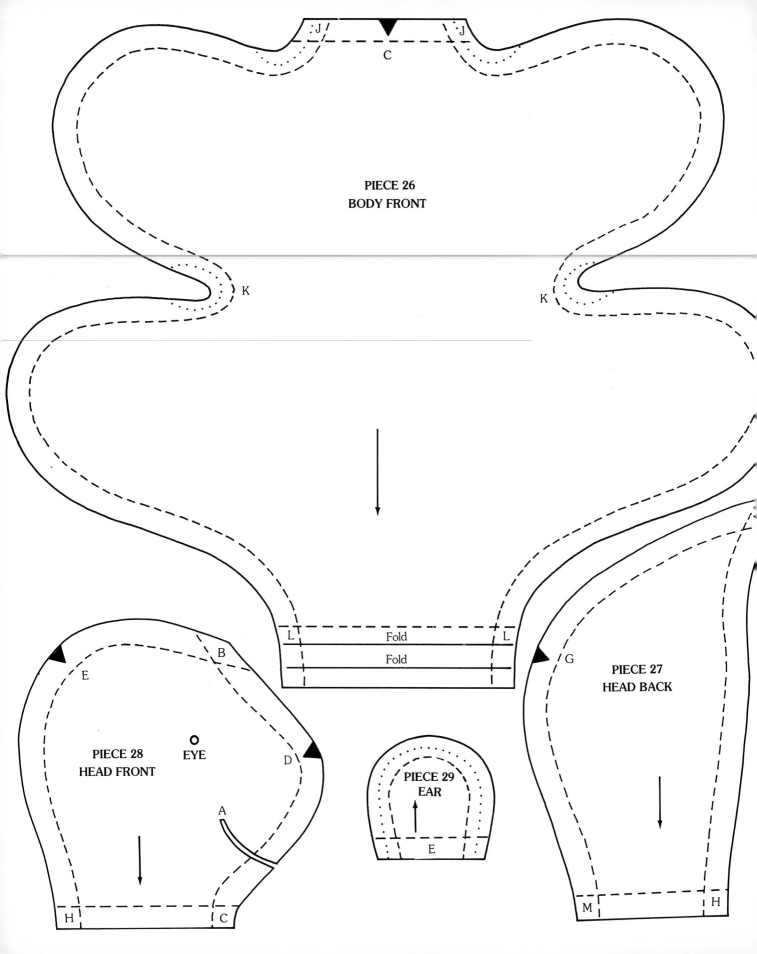

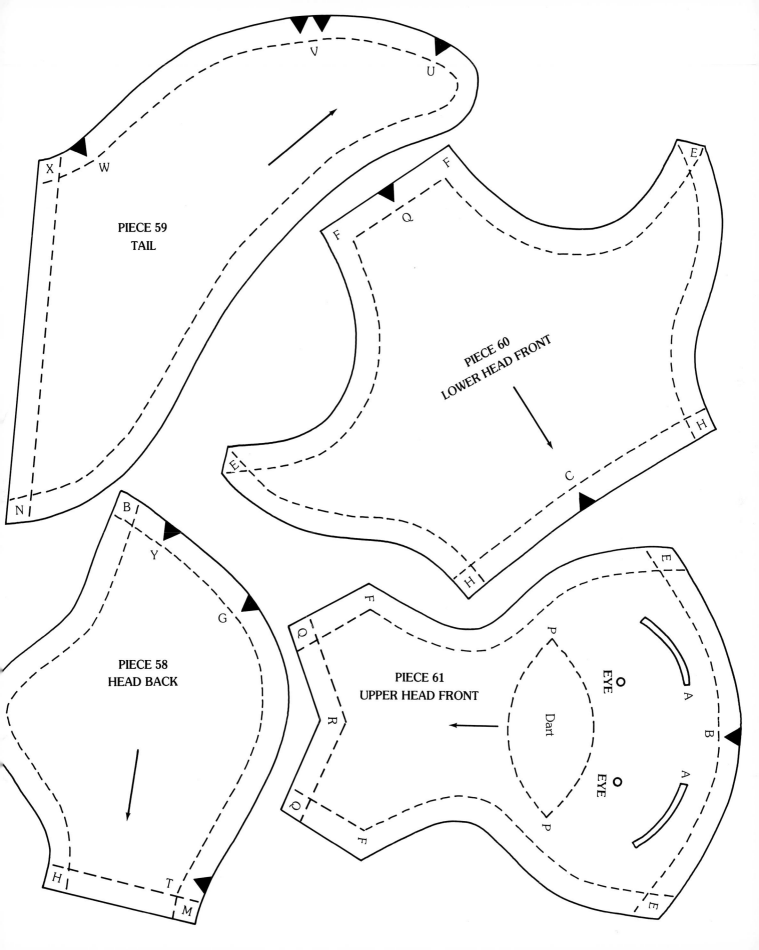

PIECE 59
TAIL

PIECE 60
LOWER HEAD FRONT

PIECE 58
HEAD BACK

PIECE 61
UPPER HEAD FRONT

EYE

EYE

Dart

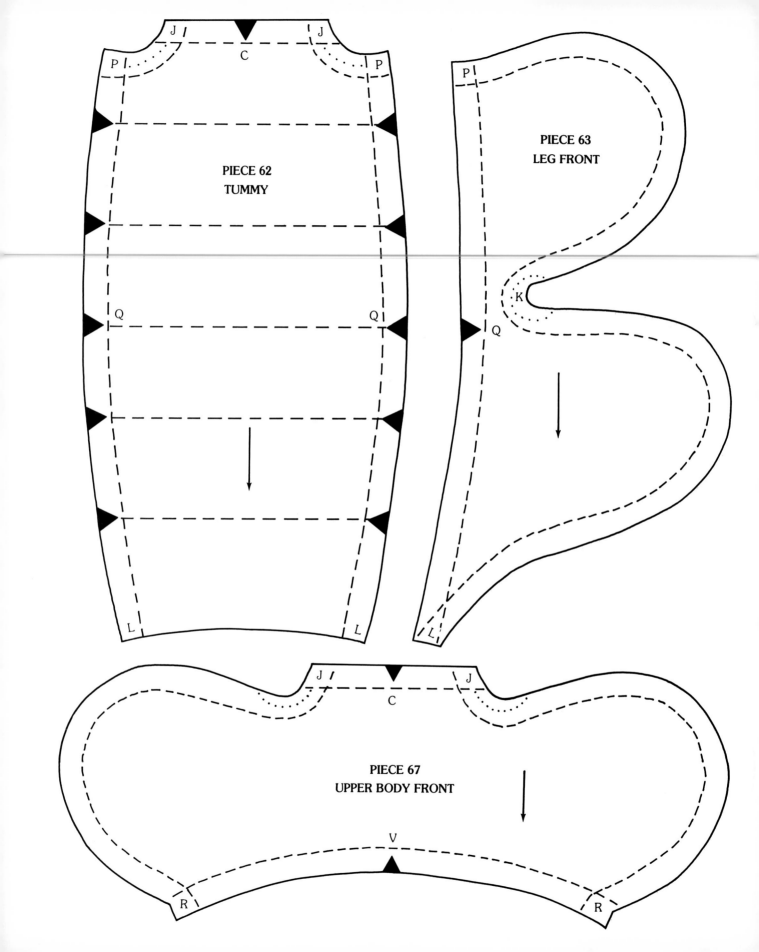

PIECE 62
TUMMY

PIECE 63
LEG FRONT

PIECE 67
UPPER BODY FRONT

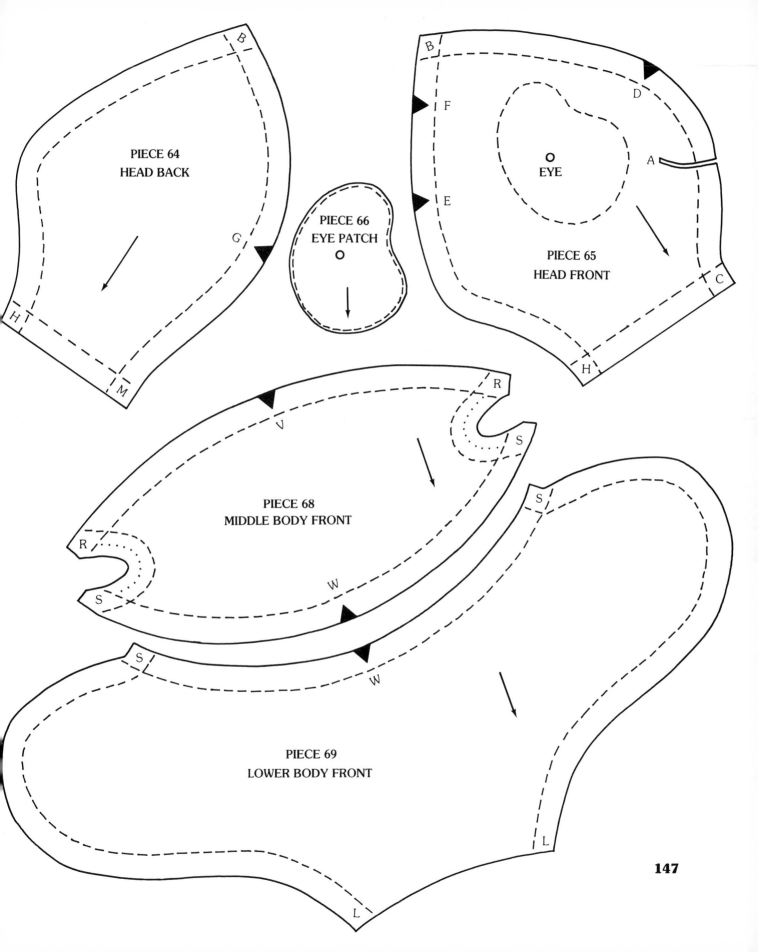

PIECE 64
HEAD BACK

PIECE 66
EYE PATCH

EYE

PIECE 65
HEAD FRONT

PIECE 68
MIDDLE BODY FRONT

PIECE 69
LOWER BODY FRONT

147

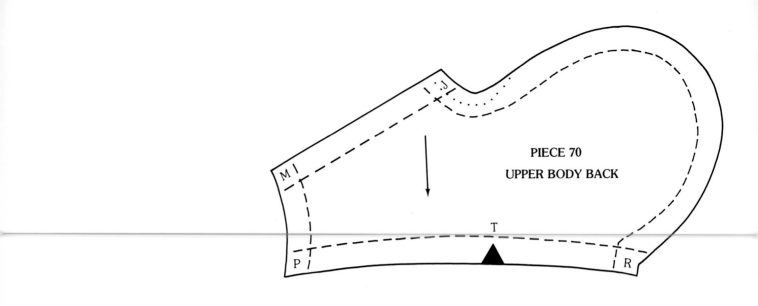

PIECE 70
UPPER BODY BACK

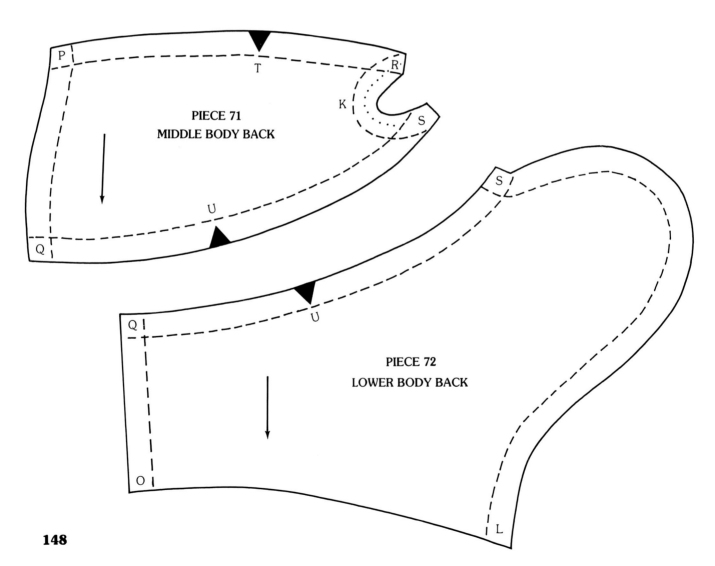

PIECE 71
MIDDLE BODY BACK

PIECE 72
LOWER BODY BACK

148

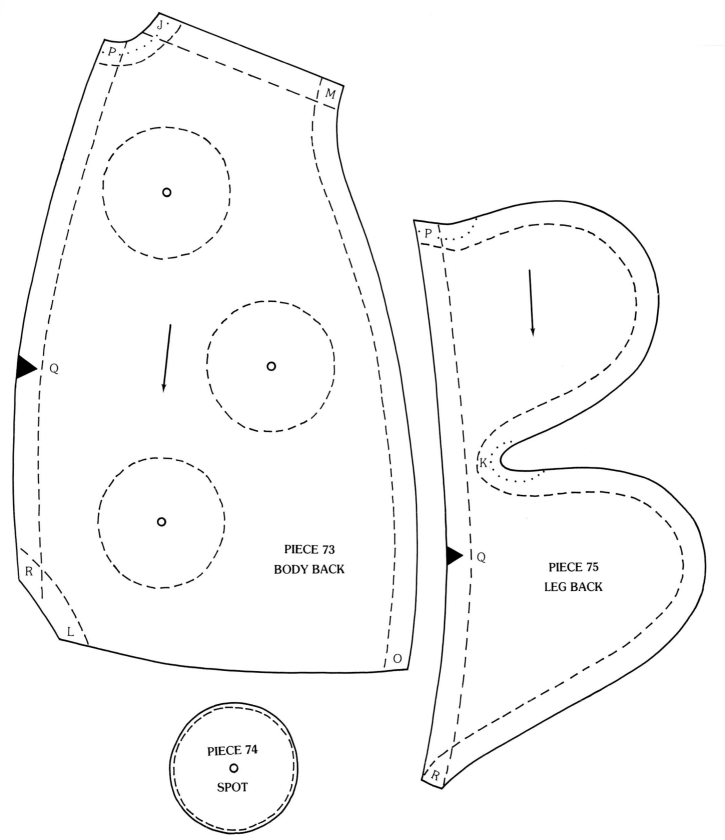

PIECE 73
BODY BACK

PIECE 74
SPOT

PIECE 75
LEG BACK

149

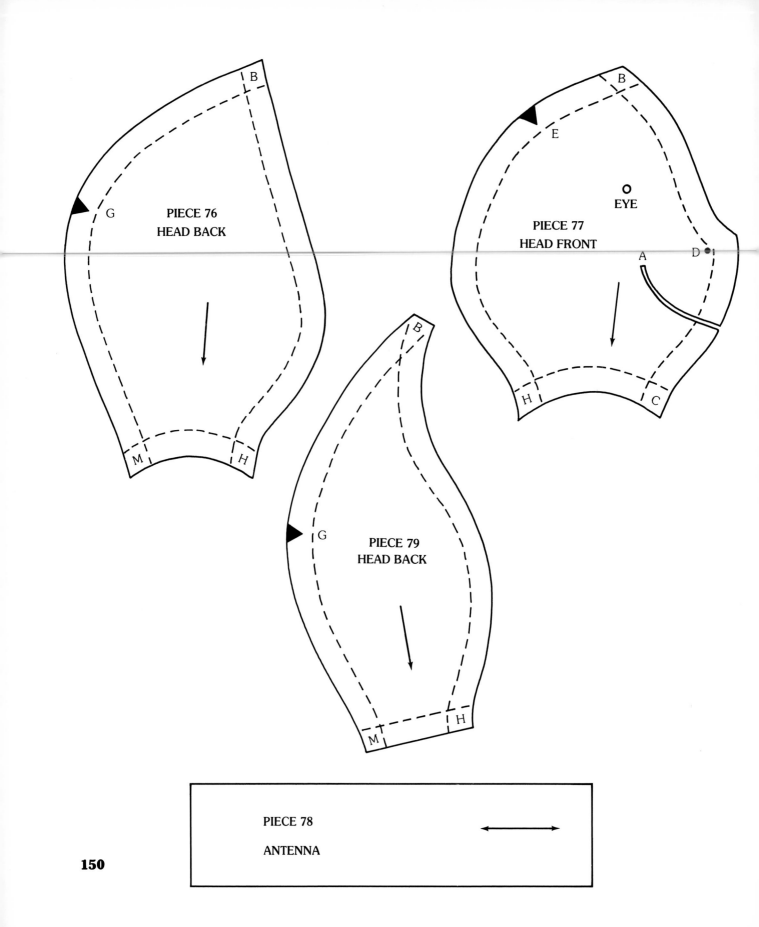

PIECE 76
HEAD BACK

B

G

M H

PIECE 77
HEAD FRONT

B

E

O
EYE

A D

H C

PIECE 79
HEAD BACK

B

G

M H

PIECE 78

ANTENNA

150

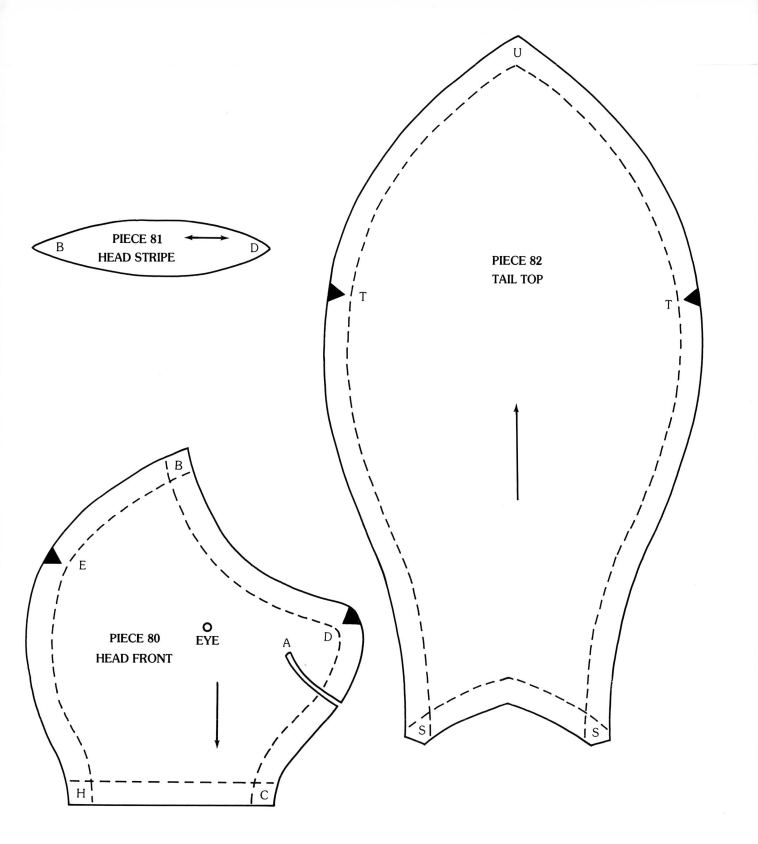

PIECE 81
HEAD STRIPE

B   D

PIECE 82
TAIL TOP

U

T   T

S   S

PIECE 80
HEAD FRONT

EYE

B

E

A   D

H   C

151

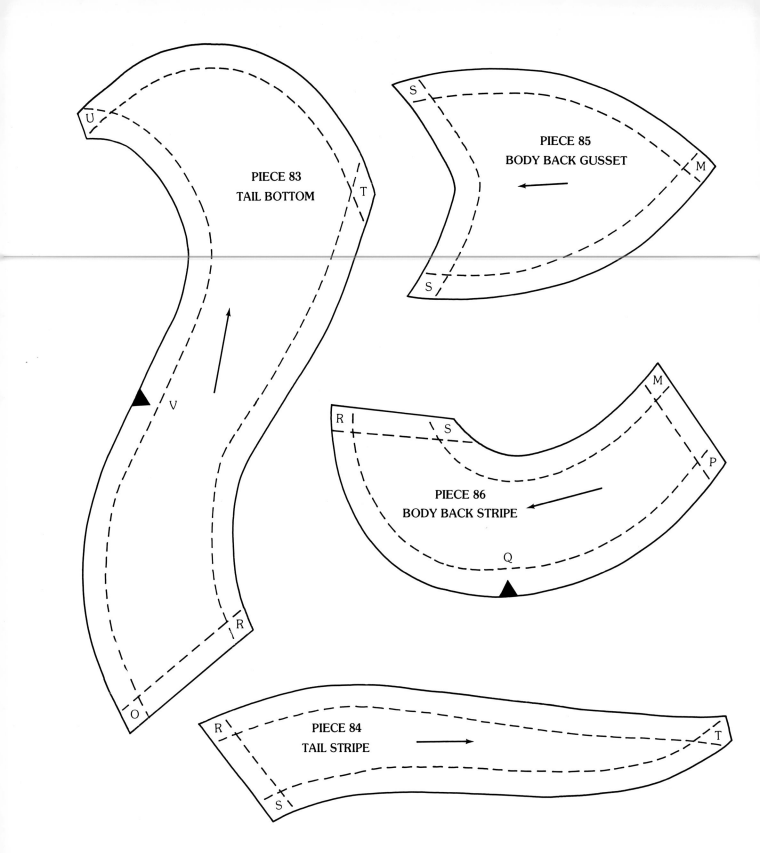

PIECE 83
TAIL BOTTOM

U

T

V

R

O

PIECE 85
BODY BACK GUSSET

S

M

S

PIECE 86
BODY BACK STRIPE

R

S

M

P

Q

PIECE 84
TAIL STRIPE

R

S

T

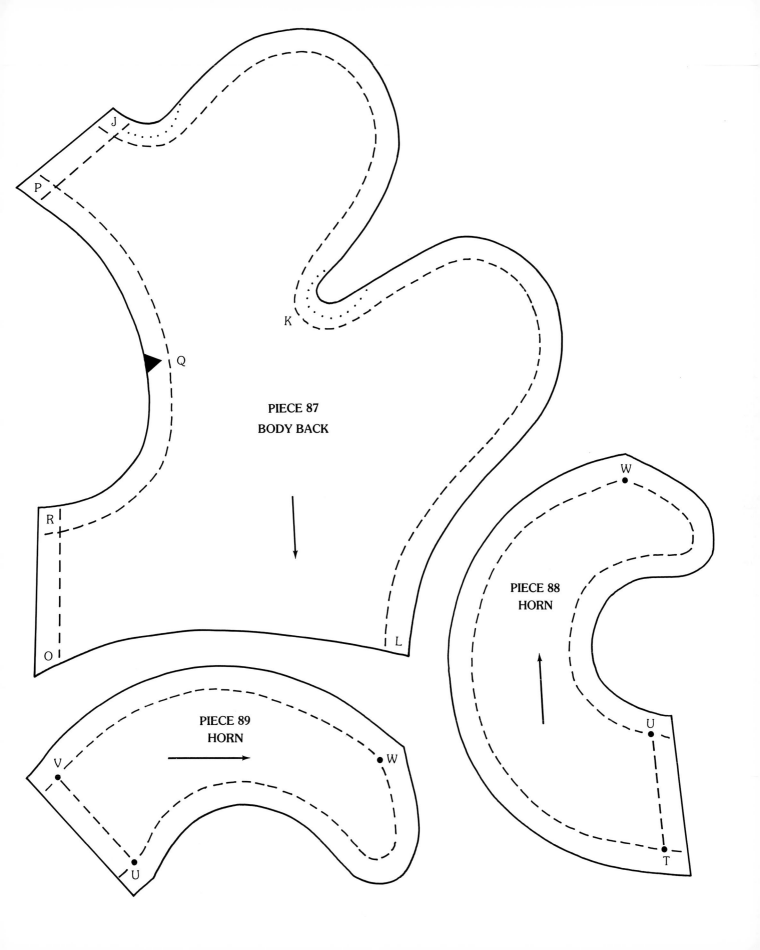

PIECE 87
BODY BACK

PIECE 88
HORN

PIECE 89
HORN

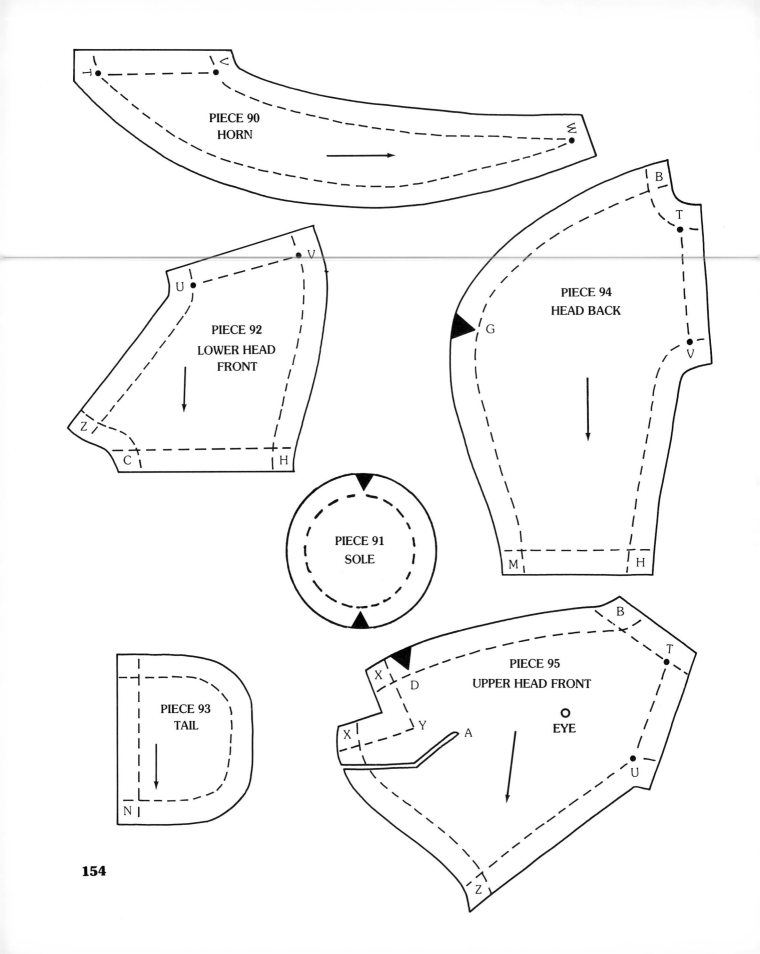

PIECE 90
HORN

PIECE 94
HEAD BACK

PIECE 92
LOWER HEAD
FRONT

PIECE 91
SOLE

PIECE 93
TAIL

PIECE 95
UPPER HEAD FRONT

EYE

154

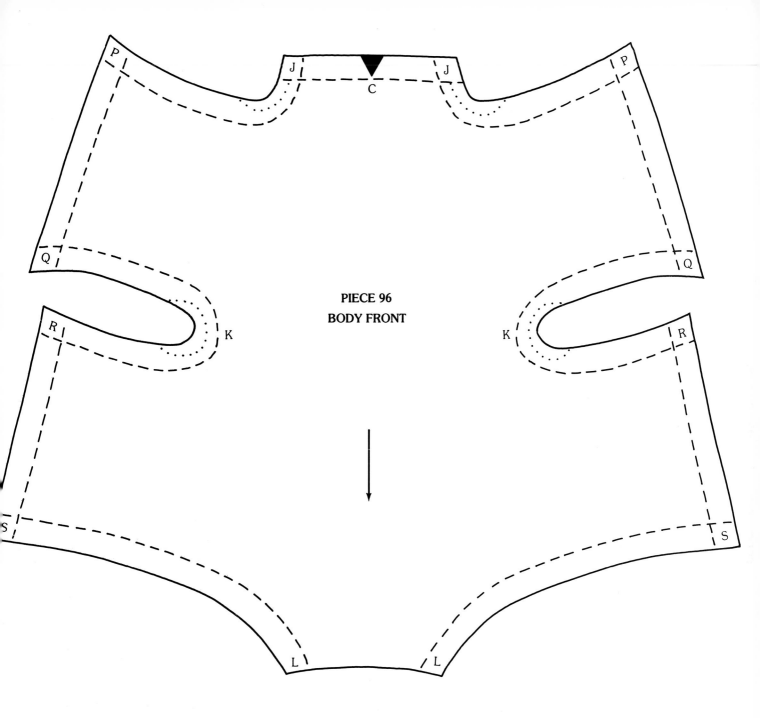

PIECE 96
BODY FRONT

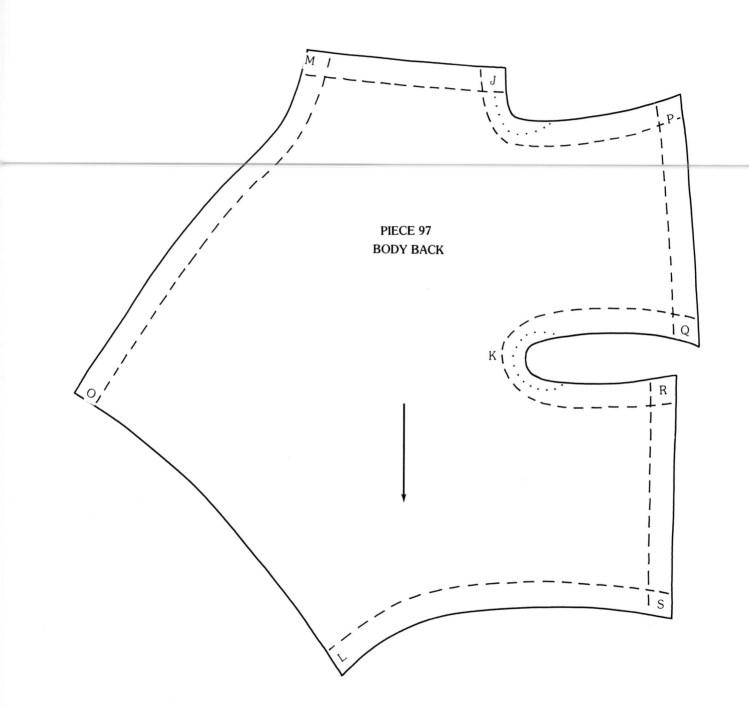

PIECE 97
BODY BACK

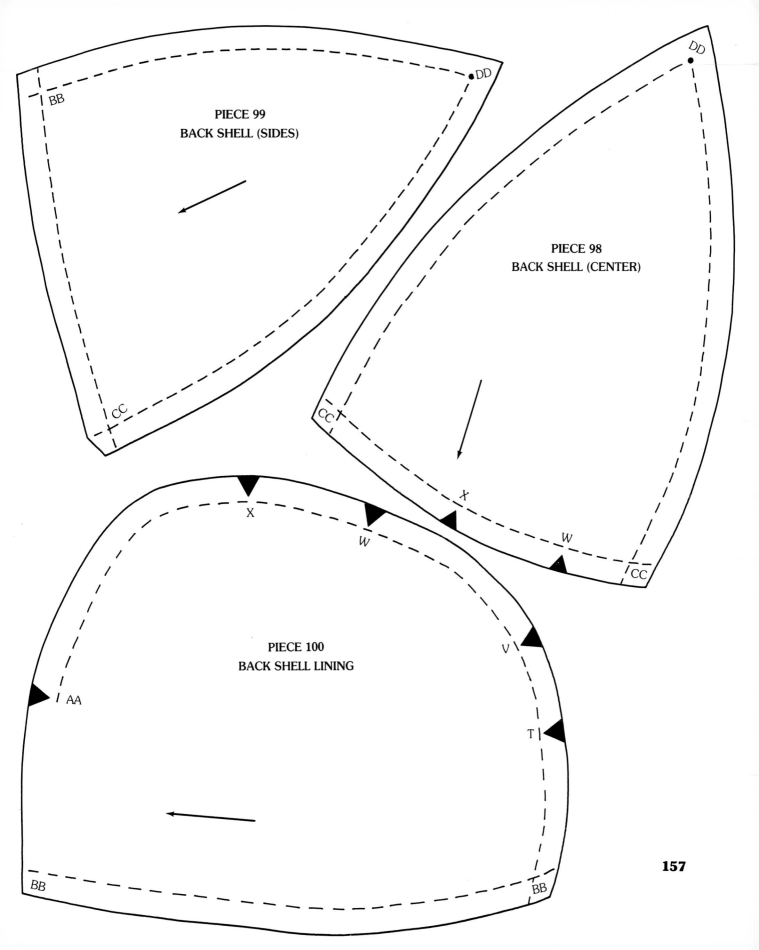

PIECE 99
BACK SHELL (SIDES)

BB

DD

CC

PIECE 98
BACK SHELL (CENTER)

CC

X

W

CC

DD

PIECE 100
BACK SHELL LINING

X

W

V

AA

T

BB

BB

157

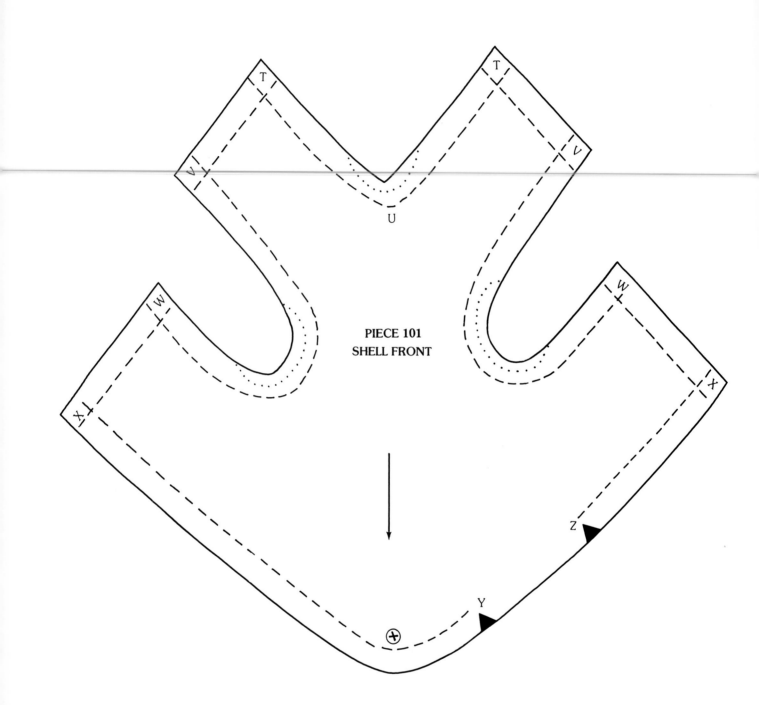

PIECE 101
SHELL FRONT

158

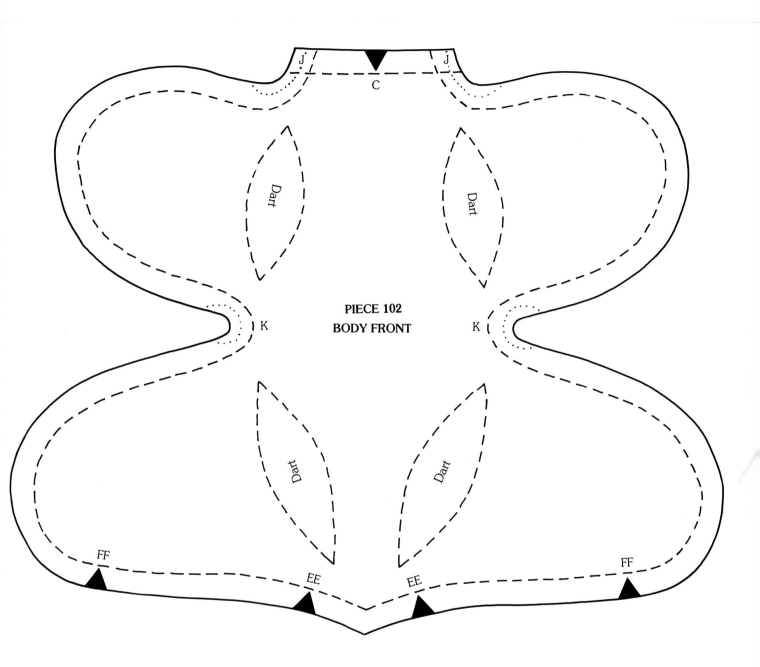

PIECE 102
BODY FRONT

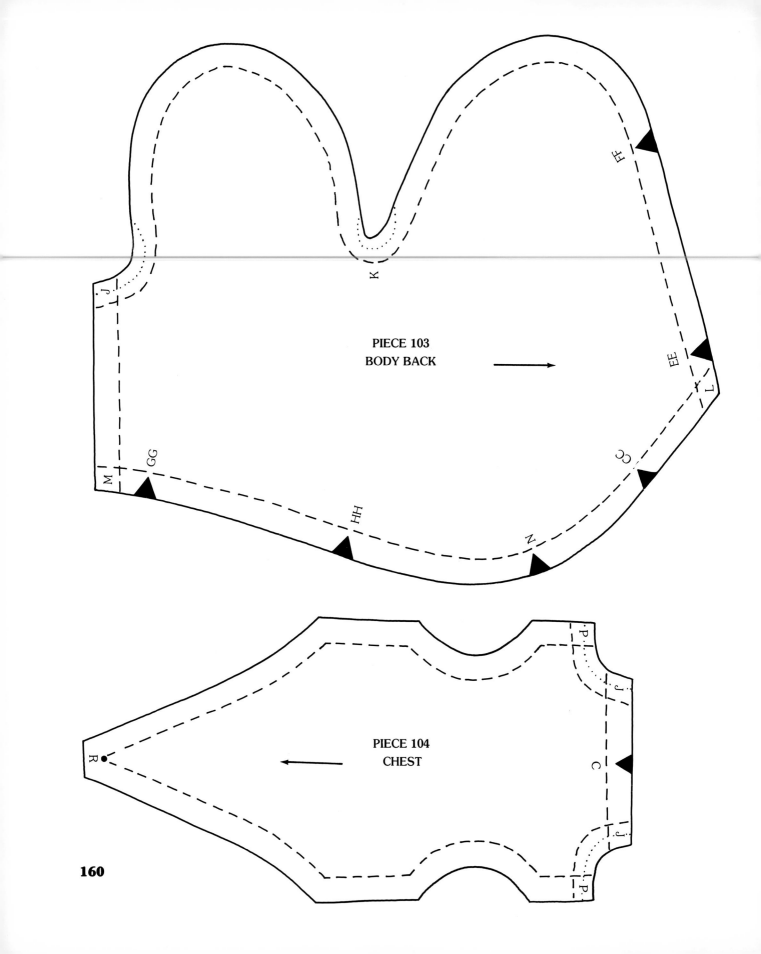

PIECE 103
BODY BACK

K

J

FF

EE

L

GG

CC

M

HH

N

PIECE 104
CHEST

R

P

J

C

J

P

160

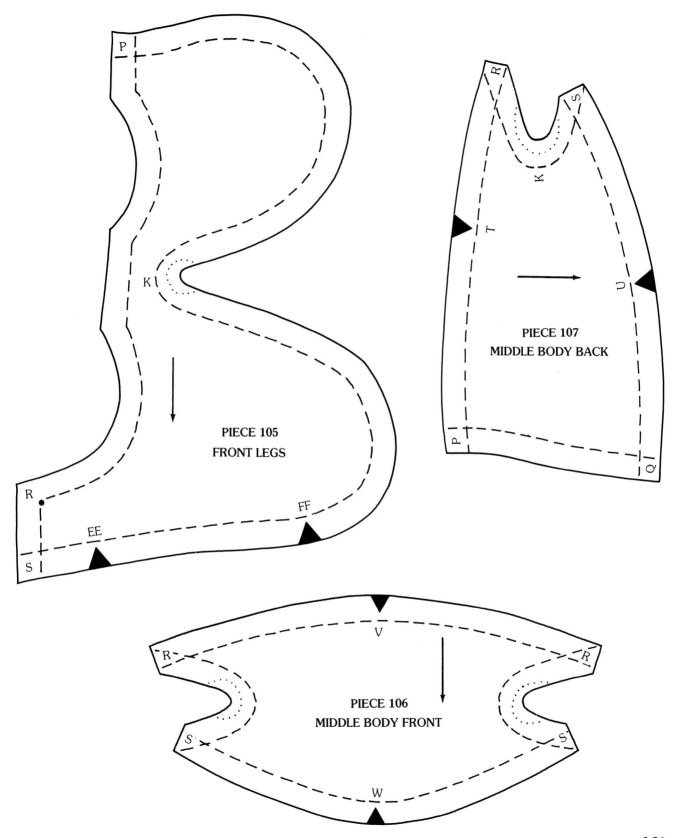

PIECE 105
FRONT LEGS

PIECE 107
MIDDLE BODY BACK

PIECE 106
MIDDLE BODY FRONT

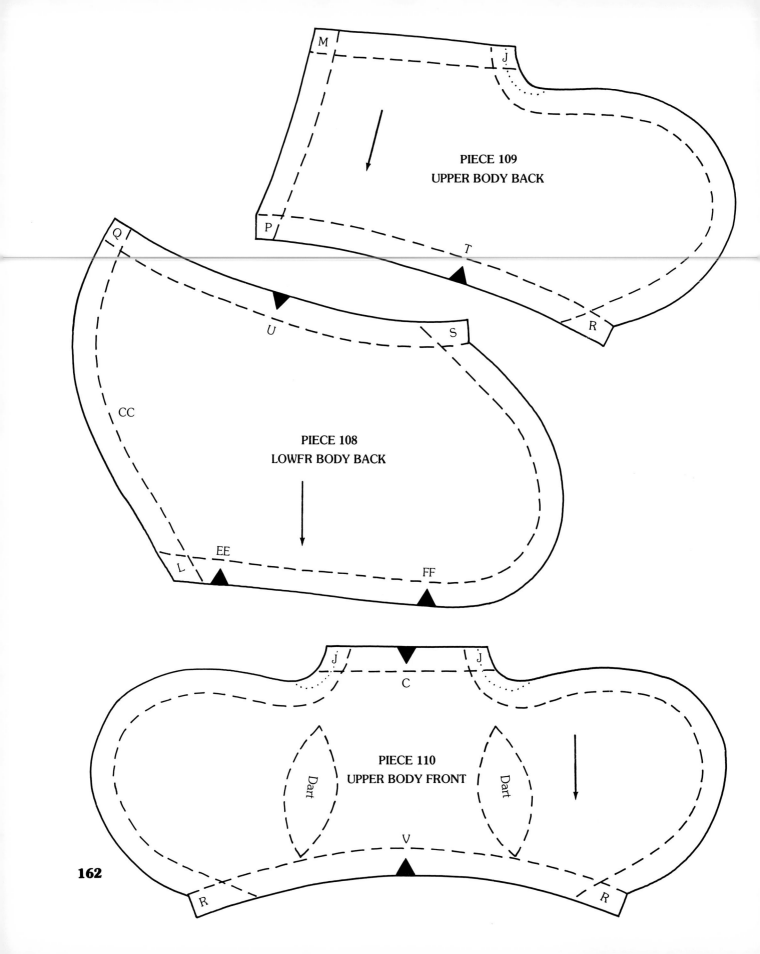

PIECE 109
UPPER BODY BACK

PIECE 108
LOWFR BODY BACK

PIECE 110
UPPER BODY FRONT

Dart

Dart

162

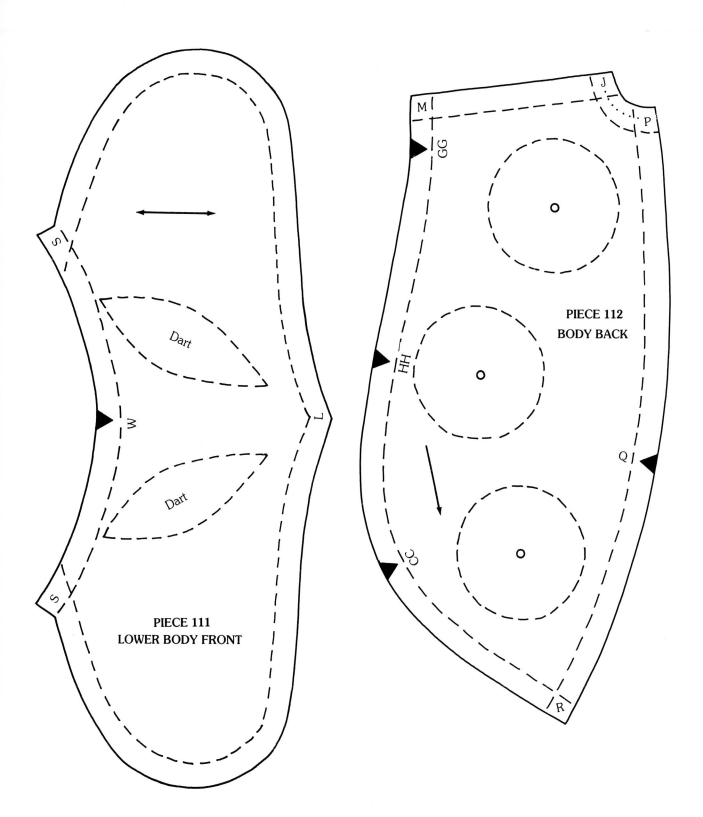

PIECE 111
LOWER BODY FRONT

Dart

Dart

S

W

S

L

PIECE 112
BODY BACK

M

J

GG

P

HH

Q

CC

R

163

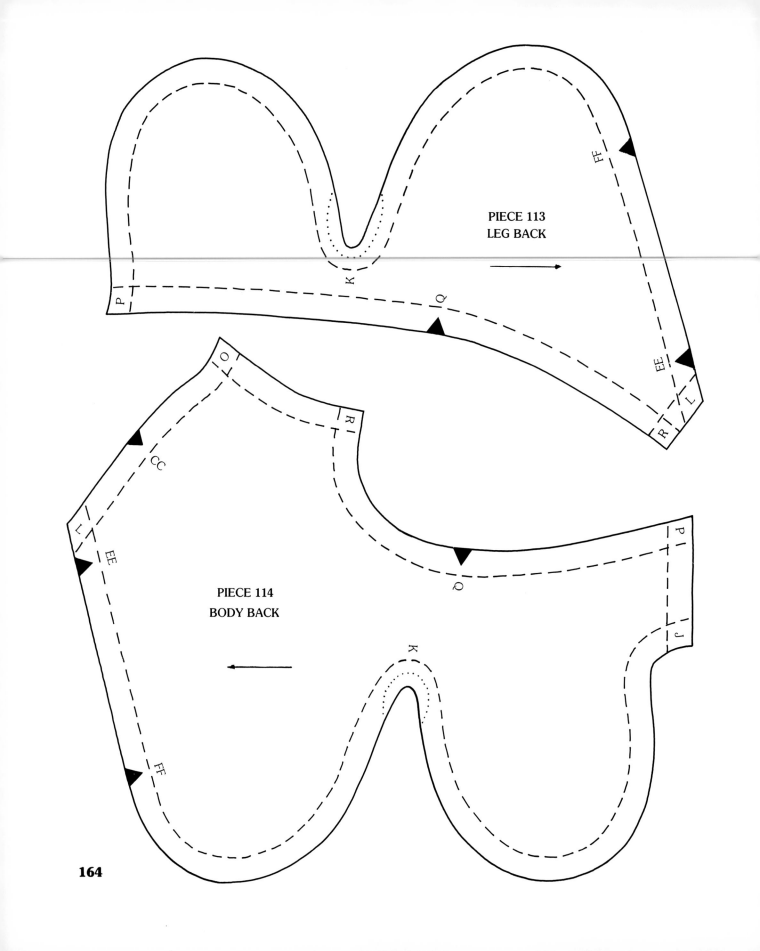

PIECE 113
LEG BACK

PIECE 114
BODY BACK

164

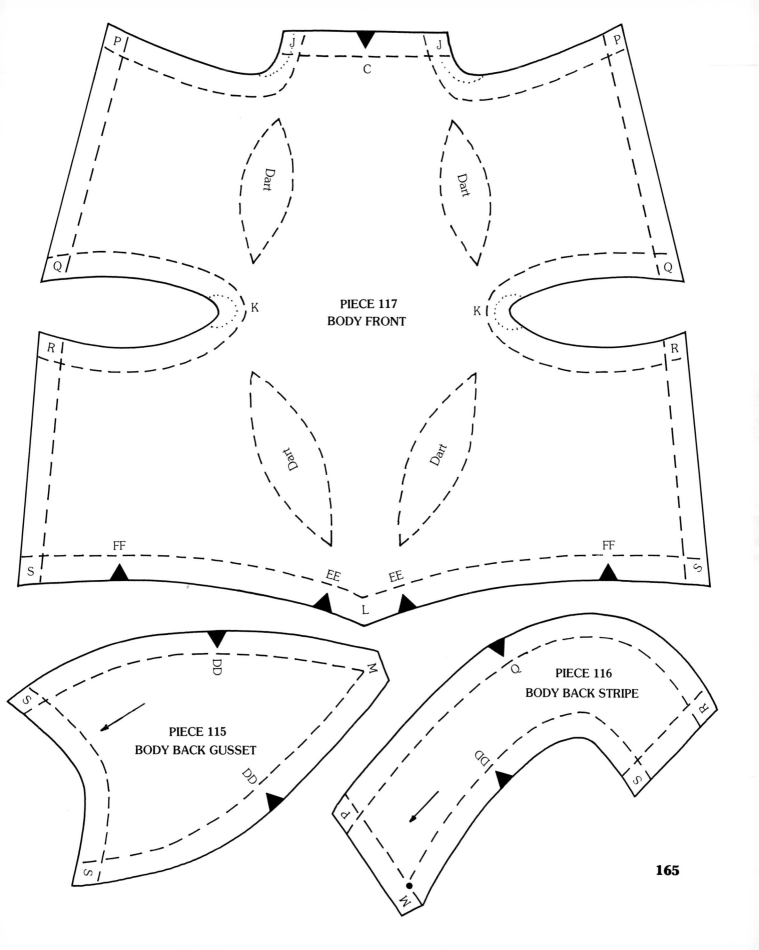

PIECE 117
BODY FRONT

PIECE 115
BODY BACK GUSSET

PIECE 116
BODY BACK STRIPE

165

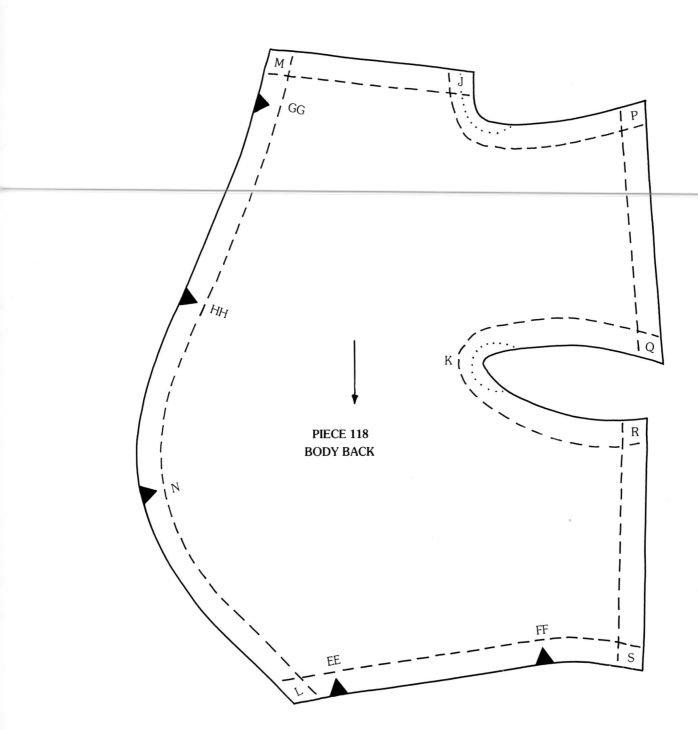

PIECE 118
BODY BACK

Index

For information on how you can have *Better Homes and Gardens* delivered to your door, write to: Mr. Robert Austin, P.O. Box 4536, Des Moines, IA 50336.